POETRY NOW SOUTH & SOUTH WEST ENGLAND 2004

Edited by

Chiara Cervasio

First published in Great Britain in 2004 by
POETRY NOW
Remus House,
Coltsfoot Drive,
Peterborough, PE2 9JX
Telephone (01733) 898101
Fax (01733) 313524

All Rights Reserved

Copyright Contributors 2004

SB ISBN 1 84460 849 2

FOREWORD

Although we are a nation of poets we are accused of not reading poetry, or buying poetry books. After many years of listening to the incessant gripes of poetry publishers, I can only assume that the books they publish, in general, are books that most people do not want to read.

Poetry should not be obscure, introverted, and as cryptic as a crossword puzzle: it is the poet's duty to reach out and embrace the world.

The world owes the poet nothing and we should not be expected to dig and delve into a rambling discourse searching for some inner meaning.

The reason we write poetry (and almost all of us do) is because we want to communicate: an ideal; an idea; or a specific feeling. Poetry is as essential in communication, as a letter; a radio; a telephone, and the main criterion for selecting the poems in this anthology is very simple: they communicate.

CONTENTS

My Mum	Ashleigh Rice	1
Trying To Write	Tim Browse	2
Ode To Village Life, Corfe Castle, Dorset	Gillian Humphries	3
Institutionalisation	Sandra Simmons	4
Electric Brae	A Quinn	5
Wartime In Dorset	John Paulley	6
Happiness	Sammy Michael Davis	7
Down And Out Near Taunton	Jësu Ah'so	8
In A Hurry!	Peter R Beadle	9
Words Like Thorns	Michael S Selhi	10
A Day's Outing	Gaynor Barry	11
Out Of The Frying Pan	Judy P Keenan	12
Netley Abbey, Hampshire	Stephen Morley	13
Me - The Coward	Dorothy Winters	14
When You Smile	Andrew Williams	15
The Slayer Of Mysteries	G Watson	16
The Football Ground	Jenny Winkworth	17
The Quintessential Miracles	Beulah Walters	18
Orange Ball	Paula Ann Savage	19
Birthday Poem	Louise Knight	20
Under The Sun	Joe David	21
When What Once Was	Kevin Ryan	22
The Rainbow's End	CWW	23
A Paean To My Love	Maurice Coles	24
In The Garden	Christine Stallion	25
Hannah's Gift	Vera Perrott	26
You Died	Amy E Pluess	27
A Lifetime Gone	Angie Tuppen	28
L'Amour	Ann Hubbard	29
Conflagration	Rex Baker	30
Just A Thought	Ursula Macdonald	31
Poetry In Motion	Annette Foreman	32
Untitled	L Ives	33
Concorde	Marie Ashford	34

Please No Peas!	Mary Grace	35
Cats And Poets	Tim Sharman	36
Why?	Pauline Perks	37
Before It Is Too Late	Elaine Priscilla Kilshaw	38
Awakening	Marina Trowell	39
Spitbank Fort	Pauline Horsham	40
The Lavender Fields	Richard Gould	41
Gillian, My Sister	Barry Ryan	42
Auntie Gillian	Hannah Ryan	43
People's Ordonnance Emanating Tenderness; Sincerity	William Johnson Lyth	44
Checkout	Fraser Hicks	45
And Me?	Moya Hastings	46
Realising Ambition	Ron Powell	47
Softness	George Potten	48
Goodnight, My Nan	Victoria Morley	49
Swanage Pier, Swanage, Dorset, England	Carol Ann Darling	50
Garden Of Many Flowers	Celia Meaker	51
Summer Days	Carol Anne Crompton	52
Creature Of The Night	Rosemary Barter	53
Light	Ian Williams	54
The Lost Gardens Of Heligan	Jane Clay	55
Bedtime Prayer	Philippa Howard	56
That Funny Cat	Sebastian Bird	57
Gloucester City	Jeannie Ashplant	58
Lost	Robert Townsend	59
Walking Home	Neil Warren	60
The Slimmed Down . . .	Edward James Williams - A Bystander Poet	61
Chardonnay Flows	Steven J Smith	62
A Spring Night	Caroline Smith	63
So Welcome	Sally-Anne Hardie	64
The Lover's Dream	Emma Chapman	65
Don't Stand And Stare	Margaret Ward	66
Conflict Of Emotion	M A Beckett	67
Alone	Robert Humphrey	68
Scrumping	Patricia Mackenzie	70

Kneeling	George Coombs	71
To The Suffering In Africa	Katherine Corson	72
For The Moment	Mark Anthony Games	73
Country Life	J Williams	74
The West Pier	Irene Snatt	75
Cockney Rhyming Slang	Stella Haynes	76
The Lighthouse	Maureen Ashing	77
The Good Old Days!	Dorothy M Parker	78
My Day Off	Rowena	79
Untitled	Ruth King	80
Cardboard City	Graham Jones	81
Capture The Imagination	Amy Stamp	82
Strawberry Snow	Patricia Adele Draper	83
Thoughts On Kent	Michael D Swift	84
Second Chances	Leah O'Connor	85
Dungeness	Jax Burgess	86
Home At Last	June Edridge	88
Untitled	P W Corbett	89
Down In The Valley	Jack Scrafton	90
Dare	C S Rowland	91
Ladder Of Life	Lyn Budd	92
My Valentine	Patricia Turner	93
Make A Stand	Vicki Billinghurst	94
The Evacuee	Doreen Simson	95
One Step Forward And Two Steps Back	Caroline Charman	96
So Close But Far	B Manhire	97
Autumn Acorns	Connie Laurent	98
Darren	Vicky Jones	99
Training Antics	Edith Buckeridge	100
The Unfortunate Slip Up	Wendy Orlando	101
The Office Boy	E M Housman	102
Slow Decline	Gillian Maynard	103
Lust	Bob Crossley	104
Dreaming	Veronica E Terry	106
Lazy Sea	Susan E Roffey	107
May And Me	Sylvia Connor	108
Freedom	Jan Cowper-Smith	109

A Scorned Soul	Hannah Pay	110
Make The Move!	John L Wright	111
Handwriting - A Lost Art	Margaret Ann Wheatley	112
New Year	Becky Morris	113
A Little Time With Me	Suzy Verma	114
Shhhh!	Gerasim	115
Seasons Of Life	Beth	116
Herb Woman	Sarah Williams	117
Shadow	Liam Satchell	118
Words Of Love	Tim Weeks	119
Tears Of Joy	Esta Taylor	120
Churches! Cricket And Carnival!	Rachel Mary Mills	121
Christmas For Us	D R Webber	122
Toe The Line	Michelle Cunningham	123
A Catechism	Jillian Mounter	124
Memory Garden	Pey Colborne	126
Tell Me?	Kyra Louise Reynolds	128
Is Earth Bursting?	M D Bedford	129
Coming Home In Winter	AnnMarie Eldon	130
The Holocaust	Alex Edwards	131
Freedom	Yvonne Bulman-Peters	132
May Display	Olive Homer	133
Ode To A Man With A Musical Gait	Lynne O'Connor	134
Numbers	Stephen Paul	135
Cider	Pam Redmond	136
First Snow	Janet L Smith	137
Goodbye	Rosanna Anstice	138
A Visit From Our Daughter	Carole Ann Catt	139
The Overview	Lou	140
Women	Robert Reddy	141
The Storm!	Gemma Musgrove	142
Tom At Tintagel	Linda Bond	143
Milverton	Sylvie Johnstone	144
Our Somerset 2004	Robin Cherry	145
Blackthorn Winter	Penny Allwright	146
Death Of Romance	Jennie Gilbert	147
Miaow Miaow	Violet Higgins	148

The Kite	Doris M Miller	149
Circles	Estelle Ann Emily Jackson	150
Somerset 2004 - ...	Paul Spender	151
The Promise	R Bryant	152
A Computer Widow	Rosemary Davies	153
The Engagement	Anabel Green	154
Sister Dear	Beverly Maiden	155
Life's Journey	Brian Muchmore	156
Urban Hunter Gatherer	Mark Sherborne	157
Bellever Summer	D M Neu	158
Sepia Giants	Martin Parker	159
Healthy And Free, The World Was Before Us!	Beryl Moorehead	160
Still Devon	James L Wood	162
Full Circle	V Jean Tyler	163
Return To Devon	Jerry Dowlen	164
The Frontline	R S Wayne Hughes	165
Special Moments	Dawn Woon	166
Blessings	Olive Young	167
Perranuthnoe	Sallie Boothman	168
In-Between Times	Alan M Kent	169
Welcome To Cornwall	Jim Pritchard	170
To Kill A Fox	Eve M Turner	172
Self Defence	Kailie Old	173
The All Night Diner	David Waddilove	174
Hollow Laughter	Jane Clarke	175
Sleepless	Jacqueline Briggs	176
Conversation With A Tree	Talmadge Rogalla	177

My Mum

I love writing poems
it's really fun
I love writing poems
and this one's about my mum

She's really kind
she makes the rule
and I think you will find
she's really cool

She's loving and caring
kind and sweet
funny and sharing
and very neat

She makes me laugh
she cures me when I'm ill
she makes me have a bath
and she pays the bill

Sometimes she gets mad
and shouts at me
she makes me sad
but she still loves me

She is the best
my bestest chum
better than the rest
and she's *my mum.*

Ashleigh Rice (11)

TRYING TO WRITE

I've tried my hand at poetry,
And boy it really sucks.
When asked to be original,
My words run out of luck.

I can plagiarise and steal,
Copy and broadly hint,
But when the too too solid flesh doth melt,
It causes quite a stink!

My rhythm can't flow smoothly,
My meaning can't be condensed into the
Correct number of syllables required.
My lines can never rhyme,
Or be in time like other poets; you see?

My sombre poems are laughable,
My silly ones sincere.
If I try to make 'em funny,
All people do is sneer.

Yet still I write, and so I shall,
Until the day I die.
If monkeys can write Shakespeare,
The least I can do is try.

Tim Browse

ODE TO VILLAGE LIFE, CORFE CASTLE, DORSET

We love to live in Corfe because it has that unique feel.
Perhaps it's down to those we meet; that's part of its appeal.
The 'Common' is our meeting point with dogs of every breed
Their owners pass the time of day, while hounds run off the lead.

Dogs walked, tasks done, we pay a call, deposit business mail.
Brief chat to Ian, our postmaster, whose help's there without fail.
A *glorious* fragrance wafts across from yonder baker's shop.
There's Nigel Dragon dripping flour, we simply have to stop!

To buy the buns and bread and cakes, they really are a treat,
With all those calories consumed, that's everyone replete.
So next we pay a call on Clealls, the friendly village store,
You're guaranteed best quality, an ever-open door.

The view of Purbeck that is seen; the climb is worth the puff,
Corfe Castle's view is seen for miles, for us that's quite enough.
This history piled in ancient rocks stands out defiantly,
For Cromwell didn't wipe it out, it's there for all to see.

Our friends in Corfe have qualities; there is a fine rapport,
We're glad to feel at one with them; there's mutual support.
So thank you one and all, you see, you're valued beyond measure.
In fact this strong community in Britain is a treasure!

Gillian Humphries

INSTITUTIONALISATION

They say that you've lost your mind
Wasn't it yours to give away?
They say that I've lost you
Did you ever belong to me?
They say you'll soon recover
But I can see you slowly drowning
While I stand here
Watching and bleeding.

Sandra Simmons

ELECTRIC BRAE

Odd behaviour isn't new to me
Odd things do seem to happen to me
But, to freewheel uphill, you must agree
Is odd behaviour, that's what happened to me.
'Tis justice to freewheel to the bottom of hill
But, there was I, pedalling like mad, with a will
Determined to reach the bottom of the Electric Brae
Like thousands before me, stubborn, thoughts in disarray
I had pedalled hard to reach the bottom of the hill
Turned round, freewheeled to the top, effort nil
Going down, you're going up
Going up, you're going down
But I certainly know when *I'm* looking up!
And I certainly know when I'm looking down.
Mind you, I was wrong about *Alan Shepherd,*
Looking up at me from the *moon!*

A Quinn

WARTIME IN DORSET

The radio broadcast came at eleven,
The country at war, all sixes and sevens;
Within minutes the sirens resounded so loud,
A plane droned above us, lost in the clouds.

My dad did his duty by joining Home Guard,
He did his night duties after working so hard;
He guarded local station with four-prong and gun,
At exercises and parades they prepared for the Hun.

In September 1940, dear Sherborne was hit,
Some 300 bombs in minutes caused fits;
Our new school had its windows all shattered to shreds,
But the comradeship, wonderful, in spite of some dead.

The voice of Churchill gave everyone a lift,
The spirits had been low, his voice was a gift;
The planes bombed our cities in dead of night,
Mum took us under table to save us a fright.

With D-Day so near the troops swarmed around,
Americans in jeeps were in county and town;
At Rushton the airfield was to play a great part,
Its gliders and troops were to pierce German hearts.

The sharing and helping throughout the long strife,
Were a model to follow in peacetime with wife;
Some bacon, some cheese, some eggs, maybe bread,
Exchanges took place, all folks they were fed.

When news of the battles brought sickness and tears,
The neighbours were splendid, did all to take fears;
Oh! Bring back that spirit of friendship and trust,
But please no more wars or we'll all eat the dust.

John Paulley

HAPPINESS

H ave a good laugh
A wake up with no cough
P ause for a thought of faith
P ut out some crumbs for the birds to be safe
I nto the daily chores with haste
N ot be unkind, but be happy instead
E arly to bed
S ee the cat or dog is fed
S leep without any fears or tears

Sammy Michael Davis

DOWN AND OUT NEAR TAUNTON

If by the station you've arrived
Ancient in its history,
Great steam engines it has seen
Think of all their mystery!
Just a stop along the way
From London down to Cornwall
Yet for one who lived here some
It doesn't make me mournful!
I lived out along the way
From Taunton Town to Chard
Eight hard years in poverty,
Outcast, banned and barred!
'His own greatest enemy,'
Is what zum zed o'me,
In Zummerzet I came to terms
With zings one zeldom zees!
A yoke of working oxen,
Hives for the Trood's bees,
Splinter groups off Elgar
Oh how zum ladies tease!
Taunton Town is elegant
The market at its hub
The police station is busy
Ah now! There's the rub!
Taunton Town zo tasty
Bloomin' in its prime
Busy bustlin' booming
Turning back hard times!
Taunton! Famous for 'fair play'?
So let it be today!

Jësu Ah'so

IN A HURRY!

Rushing, rushing, hear the sound,
People, traffic, rush around.
Tearing at tremendous speed,
No time for others to take heed.
Interested only in where they're going,
Irritated by traffic slowing.
Others always in the way,
Roadworks causing more delay.
Where are all these people going?
I really have no way of knowing.
Each one has a destiny,
I wonder where, in eternity?

Peter R Beadle

WORDS LIKE THORNS

Some people say such things to you:
words which really get to you
like a thorn in your side.
And if you fight against them they just
push the thorn in further.

You have to let the words
fly past you in the air and hope
one day they'll disappear.
The more you put your shield up
the more you'll suffer.

It's like being beaten up, and not
expecting to lose, and always
getting up only to be
knocked down again.

If you're the loser,
or pretend that you've lost,
they might walk away from you.
Otherwise you will stay in their sights.

One day a word will get through your shield
if you don't just let it pass by.
One day your opponents will fire words
like an arrow to penetrate the fortress of your heart.
The adrenaline will pump so hard
your heart will explode with anger.

Michael S Selhi

A Day's Outing

The sun is out, you can tell
The wardrobe's been raided, the shops as well!
Last year's shorts, T-shirts and sandals
Straw bags for the beach with stout leather handles.
They're there on the beach with the suntan oil
It says on the label, 'Do Not Boil'.
Out comes the Frisbee, beach ball and all,
Watch what you're doing, 'pride comes before a fall'.
Stretching and running and looking athletic
Tomorrow you'll say, 'My God, how pathetic.'
Out comes the cool bag, plastic cup and thermos
The great British picnic is once again with us.
It's time to spend hours, sat in the car,
Bumper to bumper, but this will not mar
The feeling of freedom, crawling along
The cassette player playing our favourite song.
Time to park and set up camp
'No, not there dear, the ground's a bit damp.'
Set out the deckchairs, put up the windbreaker
It's blowing a gale but that does not matter.
It's time to relax and perhaps have a natter
Who are those people making that clatter?
It's time to get moving, head for home now
Look in the field, that cow's lying down.
It's been a good day
We've all caught the sun
Oh! Well, that's another Bank Holiday gone.

Gaynor Barry

OUT OF THE FRYING PAN

Callie Simpson was a stunner in every single way.
Wolf whistles followed her to work every single day.
Energetic, full of fun, with many a joke in store,
Company she never lacked, she had friends galore.
But poor Callie had a problem - one she couldn't master
She'd set her sights on handsome Tim, the boy all the girls were after.
To reach the heart, her mum had said,
One did not have to be just good in bed
Other skills were needed too, to keep a man intent and merry.
Feed his spirit and his belly.
The problem was she couldn't cook,
Or make sense of a cookery book.
After much thought the answer was simple
It made Callie show a dimple,
Invite him round to make up a foursome seemed proper,
Hoping she wouldn't come a cropper.
Order from the takeaway,
Delivered early would save the day.
Transferred from silver foil to dish,
Produced with flourish was the wish.
The evening went just as she'd planned,
But Lady Fate reached down a crooked hand,
Despite the candlelight and wit
As hostess there she had to sit
Watching her life twist and bend,
Tim met, then married, her best friend.

Judy P Keenan

NETLEY ABBEY, HAMPSHIRE

Here beneath the creator's brilliant sky
Where the splendour of man's veneration
Perpetual folly, doth in timeless form defy
Be still, touch the calm of those whose lives were freely spent -
To his glory, and for whom there remains no sad lament.

Absent the strains of sacred melody
To rise, the fragrant air to kiss
Now but woodland song 'mongst ancient tree
Yet in prayerful form, such earthly bliss.

And vaulted stone held high as still in praise
Such faithful pose affirms a purpose clear
That awesome majesty is, with heavenly blaze
Still near.

Stephen Morley

ME - THE COWARD

Saw her fall with an awful thud
what did I do? Just stood.
Her handbag lay invitingly
just beyond her grasp.

I saw him hurry over to her
look down with smirking grin
ring in nose, ponytail and
torn jeans, he did look menacing.

Still rooted to the spot, I heard
'What you doing down there luv?'
as he pulled her to her feet
and laughing said, 'You OK dearie?'

'Yes and thanks son,' she gratefully replied.
'If you're sure, I'll be on my way.'
And whistling, off he went
leaving me, the coward, thoroughly ashamed.

Dorothy Winters

WHEN YOU SMILE

When you smile
You open up a whole new world
A world of diamonds and pearls
A world of magic unfurls
When you smile.

When you laugh
The day seems lighter
And the sun shines brighter
I want to hold you even tighter
When you laugh.

When I'm with you
I hear angels sing
With the happiness you bring
I feel like a king
When I'm with you.

Andrew Williams

THE SLAYER OF MYSTERIES

Raise your banners against me, question me, and hate me.
But you need me now, although I do not need you.
Liberators in white have unlocked my cage,
But they can no longer hold me.
I am the slayer of mysteries.

A dominion: strip-lighting sky meets sterilised earth.
Hunting grounds: a Formica plain.
Oh, but what prey to be found!
Nowhere to hide, I will discover them.
I am the slayer of mysteries.

I do not hanker for opinion; I have no compassion for faith.
A lifetime of belief counts for nothing.
Politicians may rape me, but no lawyer can dispute me.
The *only* expert witness.
I am the slayer of mysteries.

A question to feed a hypothesis
A hypothesis answered that spawns a hundred more,
But the hit of truth dulls quickly.
Stop? I cannot, will not.
I am the slayer of mysteries.

How far can I go?
I cannot answer.
Yet, if I slay them all
What then of mysteries?
Because without mystery what is life?

G Watson

THE FOOTBALL GROUND

The day is clear, the wind is bold,
But these men fear not the cold.
With spirits high they face each other
Who is that dares to call me 'Brother'?
A man in black seems to be the boss
Whistle ready for the toss.
Excitement fills the air around
This place, this pitch, this football ground.

The team in red face to the right,
They mean to fight with all their might
The home team seems to have the edge
With the crowd behind to give their pledge.
Now they wait with eager plans
To prove their greatness to the fans.
Excitement fills the air around
This place, this pitch, this football ground.

A cheer goes up as the chanting starts
Apprehension stirs through a thousand hearts
This crucial match to both the teams
Could make or break a player's dreams.
Yet only one club can take the cup
The other to settle for runner-up.
Excitement fills the air around
This place, this pitch, this football ground.

Jenny Winkworth

THE QUINTESSENTIAL MIRACLES

I see
>Sunlight flaming through half bare trees
>as leaves cascade and tumble to form russet carpet,
>while distant hills, shrouded in mist, seem unreal,
>as hot air balloon, like exclamation mark, hangs in the sky.
>The quintessential miracle of eye.

I hear
>The gamut of quacks as ducks squabble for free food,
>ears vibrate at flatness of soloist struggling for top C.
>Yet, head swims with peace at the sound of the nightingale.
>Whilst heavy exhalation of dying person means the end is near.
>The quintessential miracle of ear.

I taste
>The scrunchy crackle of fresh-ground coffee beans,
>the comforting anaesthetic relief on tooth by spicy clove.
>The sharpness of lemon, sours plums and rhubarb comes as
>a cleanser, after swallowing repulsive peanut butter - in haste.
>The quintessential miracle of taste.

I feel
>As I run barefoot, the ice-cold kiss of the frosty grass,
>the nutmeg-grater skin of a lover's unshaved features.
>Face, smarting from hot water and astringent lotion.
>The warmth emitted from hand when grasped in friendly clutch.
>The quintessential miracle of touch.

I smell
>The pungent choking fumes of modern day exhausts,
>so opposite to the seaweed tang of salty ozone.
>Yet, the musky lingering perfume of grandson's aftershave
>means more to me than words could ever tell.
>The quintessential miracle of smell.

Beulah Walters

ORANGE BALL

Raging orange ball of fire
Are you held up by the lilac hue
That floats you down to the misty horizon,
So undiluted, so pure, so true?
Don't go yet, big ball of fire,
Stay here with me and keep me warm.
With mercy I'm left with your setting promise,
I'll catch you somewhere else at dawn . . .

Paula Ann Savage

BIRTHDAY POEM

We are another year older you and me
I am a human, you are a tree
We grow and we age but in different ways.
Once a year, 24 hours a day it's quite funny
As we're never far away.
Can you believe it?
As we grow older we are growing bolder,
Well I am, I am smarter, wiser and brainier.
But as you stand still, you only know about nature.
See, there are many of you and only one of me
But we can match that by the power of three.
We are never far apart, we are always close
But just remember,
We are another year older, you and me.
I am a human, you are a tree.

Louise Knight (16)

UNDER THE SUN

Under the sun, in the sea and sand
I paddle my feet and wave my hand
At the boats that pass me by
I love the sea and the bright blue sky.
I play with my bucket and spade
I have an ice cream,
I put on sun cream,
I lay on the sand to dry
As the wind blows by.

When I go home and look out my window
I see the sun go down on the horizon.
I love the beach,
I think I will go tomorrow.

Joe David (8)

WHEN WHAT ONCE WAS

Oh children,
If we could only go back again,
For I'd rather the joy of our play than this pain,
The small, sticky hand in my hand in the rain
And Lesley and snow and the puddle-filled lane.

The summery, dusty field was so wide
Where we noisily ran with the sun on our side,
And all of the ribbons of rules were untied
And Lesley was laughing
For joy.

What strange irony must the riddle mean
That the wonder of children can only be seen
With a backward glance
But once it has gone?
Though all of the turning of days may go on . . .

Better it was with no cares to have run
Beneath the stretched arms of the very first sun,

Or when our shoes slapped the slush and our cold breath was seen
And on the black gate at dusk
I with Lesley would lean.

Kevin Ryan

THE RAINBOW'S END

Between the edge of Jane Priddy's land
And just before historic Hardway's stand,
As the contour turns to Fareham Creek's bend
Just off the shore is the rainbow's end.

Within the crook of Convict's Quay
Small boats in myriads are moored merrily,
The rainbow rests here vivid and bold
Her foot on a legendary pot of gold.

Sentinels of shelducks, seagulls and swan
Amongst those who flock here to feed upon
The low tide shore and low tide banks
Curlews, egrets, Brent geese and cormorants.

Then look to North Harbour over Fareham Creek's mouth
From ancient Caer Peris to the Sails of the South
Where Port Solent's yachts sail on splendid broad reach
And night's fairyland lights on the slopes and the beach.

Or on a silent summer evening's balm
Boats' masts are reflected in the calm
And Portsdown's glorious sunrise a golden shaft shall send
To this harbour paradise, here at the rainbow's end.

CWW

A Paean To My Love

You are the smile upon the lips of time,
The resonance beyond the bell's sweet chime,
The breeze-borne fragrance of a tropic clime,
The lilt and pattern of a lovely rhyme.
You are all tenderness, possess the charm
Of melody upon the air. Your touch is balm,
The music of your voice instils a cam
That would a wild and raging bull disarm.
You are perfection's dream of loveliness;
With all your supple shape, may I confess,
Designed to captivate; your gestures less
A movement of the limbs than a finesse
Balletic in its purity. Oh, yes,
You are sublimity made measureless –
Elusiveness your key. And you're the dream
Beyond all dreams of form and grace, the gleam
Of summer in the wintry depths. You seem
To hold perfection in your palm. Your cream
Of beauty, without peer beneath the sky,
Will hold me willing captive till I die.

Maurice Coles

IN THE GARDEN

I gaze at the statue -
Its head hung low to one side,
Sunk deep into its breast.
A bit of ivy grows here and there
Around this form that stands
At the end of the garden.
The bushes nearby are in wild
Disorder and skirt the flower beds.
The evening brings the birdsong -
To a pitch, the starlings throng in the sky.
The forlorn figure is draped by folds
Of an antique costume. Neglected decay
Laces its bedraggled majesty.
The model may have been an old sage
A bit knocked about by age.
In defiance it stands firmly on a plinth.
The stone is chipped and torn -
Its colour old and worn - while
Green mould grows everywhere.
Somehow the destruction has
Enhanced this chiselled piece.
I look and wonder for
It cannot throw off its silence.
Perhaps lovers have stood in this
Very place and gazed at the shape.
The years may have tarnished its elegance,
But it remains in the half light
A beacon to all who soldier on,
Its spirit unbroken by the wheel of time.

Christine Stallion

HANNAH'S GIFT

Hannah came to see the sea,
Hannah came and played with me,
Throwing pebbles from the shore,
Playing ducks and drakes, and more -
Running barefoot in the sand,
Picking shells with dimpled hand.
Hannah made a castle mound,
Topped it with big stones she found,
Daddy buried Hannah's feet,
Fed her sarnies - such a treat,
Mummy paddled in the sea,
Far too cold for you and me.
Then we had to say goodbye,
Goodness, how the time does fly,
When Hannah's only just turned four
And Great-aunt V's a . . . wee bit more!

Hannah called me for a kiss -
Her perfect gift, my lasting bliss.

Vera Perrott

YOU DIED

And as I held you as you died,
I felt your life slip slowly by;
It leaked as surely as your blood,
A perfect crimson in so much mud.
Your pain was such that as you lay,
You could not hear all I had to say.
Words of my love fell on unhearing ears,
Which I will regret all my years.
How cold you were, where once was warm,
Your flawless face was pale and drawn.
Your eyes were dark as ebony,
With all the hurt and agony.
And I thought that I could not bear
Your final blank and rigid stare.
And yet I found some comfort in,
The small time of your suffering.
The shock and grief will be so near,
For every day in every year.
I find some peace in that we'll be together,
For pain cannot last and love is forever.

Amy E Pluess

A Lifetime Gone

Time.
Where did it go?
Oh why did it go
So fast?

Yesterday
We were young
Our children
Unborn.

Now
We are old
Our children
Are grown.

Our world
Once simple
Now complicated
Advanced.

Years
Passed by
A lifetime
Has gone.

Angie Tuppen

L'AMOUR

A love, lost life . . .
Sight of blood was shed
The balance . . . a blade of a knife,
A body lay on the bed.
I saw, I heard, what a fright
Blackened vision.
Scream, scream held the night,
'My love,' I saw the incision.
Tension, tears.
I heard a cry
And then silence.
Tension seers,
L'amour lost sight,
I lost her in the night.

Ann Hubbard

CONFLAGRATION

I'm told the universe contains
More stars than all the grains of sand
Of every desert on the Earth.

And yet I am not moved.

I'm told within the human brain
God only knows how many cells
Conduct life's frantic business.

And yet I am not moved.

I'm told the awesome quantum world
Can manufacture paradox
And fracture logic's sovereignty.

And yet I am not moved.

I'm told they used to burn the books
Foreshadowing what I've been told,
The truth that fails to stir me.

And somehow I am moved.

Rex Baker

JUST A THOUGHT

In the silent sky,
A bird flew by
And settled in a tree.
Good it would be
If we could fly,
But with chaos in the sky
There'd be no traffic jam below,
On second thoughts,
Perhaps it's best
To bung up the roads,
Leave the birds to nest.
We could have been floating
Up to Heaven,
But, continue to suffer
On the A27.

Ursula Macdonald

POETRY IN MOTION

I will make you strong when you feel weak,
I will be the inspiration behind every single heartbeat,
I will be the helping hand that pulls you back upon your feet.

When you feel hungry I shall be the food you eat,
Even when I'm gone I will always be so near,
When you feel scared I will take away your fear.

When you feel angry I will calm and soothe you,
When you feel hurt I will be your pain relief,
When you feel tired I shall help you sleep,
I shall be the oxygen that will make you breathe.

I will give you all the love you need,
When you feel down I will give you hope,
I shall always be there for you,
When no one else will be around.

I will wipe away your tear before it falls upon your cheek,
I will be the spirit that you feel deep down in your soul,
I will show you respect and appreciation,
I shall value your true worth.

I shall be your destiny to make your life complete,
I will do all these things for you
And so much more.
If only I could have you back again
In my life once more.

Annette Foreman

UNTITLED

Just sitting
Sun shining
Birds singing
Children laughing
Ladies chatting
Men building
Life beginning
Souls searching
Never reaching
Life ending
Eyes streaming

L Ives

CONCORDE

We look back with pride to that special day
When Concorde first took to the air.
Its beautiful white pencil slim outline in the blue sky,
Its almost beak-like nose we spotted there.

It flew like a bird with great grace,
It flew at speeds greater than sound.
Its characteristic was its roar like a lion
Declaring its dominance of the skies.

It's been hard to say 'Adieu'
To this man-made creation,
To realise its costly upkeep and running
Meant it had to go into mothballs.

So many are saddened by its departure.
How many excuses will we find each year
In order to see this Queen of the Skies take flight
And fill us once more with delight?

Marie Ashford

PLEASE NO PEAS!

Whenever a friend asks me to tea,
There is one thing on which we must agree.
Chips are fine and pizza's great,
But please, no peas upon my plate!

They are surely my worst enemy . . .
The scourge of every party tea,
They seem so small and round and sweet,
But don't be fooled; it's pure deceit.

Whilst at Amy's sixth birthday,
I knew a pea had gone astray,
I thought, *stay calm, don't throw a fit* . . .
But then I went and trod on it.

And oh, that day with Sam and Ben,
(I cannot go there again!)
Somehow my fork just went awry . . .
And a thousand peas shot through the sky.

But the worst day of my life
Came when I swapped my fork for knife,
I thought at last I might succeed . . .
(But I well and truly 'pead'!)

Peas on table,
Peas on floor,
Peas escaping through the door.
Peas on Tiddles (he's our cat,)
Peas all over Mum's new mat.
Peas just hurtling down like hail,
(And bouncing off the picture rail.)

So I beg of you, don't let me see
A single dreaded, dratted *pea!*

Mary Grace

CATS AND POETS

Poets like cats
And cats like poets
Although cats can't read
And they always plead
For an extra morsel of food
Or a stroke for a good mood
Cats like poets who make a fuss
And bring them some huss
Poe had a black cat on his shoulder
That grew larger and bolder
On the page of Gothic mystery
Cats like a certain symmetry
Like to chase pens and paper
Cotton reels and tapers
They sometimes like to play
With an animal prey
Poets like looking in cats' eyes
And listening to contented sighs
Cats like poets until they lose the tin opener
Pat a dog, what a no hoper
Poets and cats make good friends
When they drop the mask of the pretend.

Tim Sharman

WHY?

Why does the sun stay in the sky and not fall to the ground?
Why does the breeze move past my face and never make a sound?
Why do I have to go to bed when I just want to play?
And why does Father Christmas only come on Christmas Day?
Why am I hot in summer and cold in winter snow?
The answers to these questions I think I'll never know.
My dad says not to worry when I'm sitting on his knee.
I s'pose it's cos I'm only nearly three.

Why does my mum say, 'Ask your dad,'
And Dad says, 'Ask your mum'?
Why do they get embarrassed when I ask where I came from?
How can I get an answer - I won't learn if I'm not told.
It's frustrating being nearly three years old.

Pauline Perks

BEFORE IT IS TOO LATE

Flowers, but no water
Birds have no song to sing.
No love that grows
No hope eternal.
Heritage confiscated
Truth evaporated.
Self-esteem vilified
Dreams and desires put aside
Acceptance of your word denied.
Good men banished to savage seas.
To stop us drifting on this tragic path
Let us fight with dignity
To let one and all be free
To give us back our liberty.

Elaine Priscilla Kilshaw

AWAKENING

I never thought I'd like the sea,
vast blue and curved.

I never noticed the changing colours,
I thought they were
edging away from me,
suspicious and cold.

The boats floating on the line of white hills,
slapping the face of the bow,
under the hopeful fresh-faced sky,
blushed with powder snow cheeks.

Yet the colour changed
from dawn misty noon to hazy breakthrough green,
turning dusky hewed silver
as I switched off my PC.

We sat beside seven polished white teeth,
fragrancing the warm summer breeze on the pebbled floor,
watching the man take a dip,
the children running along the
water's edge: all laughing, all warm,
looking up at the birds flying against the sea salt air.

It was as I drove round the roundabout, down towards Little Chelsea,
I stopped at the traffic lights for a lady who smiled.
I said this is home.
Relaxed.
Enjoying not resenting as the radio sang,
'Everything's gonna be fine, fine, fine'.

I drove along the sea road
and saw how it had waited for me, unchanging.
It was then that I took a dip, sat down and
smiled back.

Marina Trowell

SPITBANK FORT

You can visit our fort out at Spitbank,
Go back in time with a tour,
But it's not just another museum,
We do just a little bit more.
There's our pub night out in the Solent.
Discos and parties galore,
Pig roast, chicken and crumbles,
When you've been once,
You'll come back for more.
You can book up for lunch on a Sunday,
For your wedding or retirement do,
In fancy dress, all looking a mess,
Or prom night - it's up to you,
You can party away with the disco,
Watch the sun disappear out of view,
See the ships sailing by - the stars in the sky
Or just have a chat with the crew.
So for a quiet lunch out on a Sunday,
A night at the pub - just for two,
Parties for wedding or birthday,
Just ask, we'll accommodate you.

Pauline Horsham

THE LAVENDER FIELDS

I'm standing on this low ridge,
Beneath a gnarled old olive tree
Offering me some welcome shade
Form the fierce midday heat
Of the Mediterranean clime
Stretching out before me
Run the rows of lavender
Close at hand each has its own shape
But as they stretch away down the slope
They merge into a tide of colour
It's not all blue, as someone has had
The foresight to place some rows of white
Which serve to give a feeling
Of land-locking waves
With nowhere to rise and fall
Held as if frozen.

Richard Gould

GILLIAN, MY SISTER

Gillian is older than me,
(By two years), as she sips her tea.
Wants to watch 'Emmerdale' on the telly,
Instead must take Chester out, daily.

Over the fields, they go for a walk . . .
Bumping into other dog owners, as they talk.
'Are you the person whose cat comes too?'
They sometimes ask, whilst watching the view.

My daughter regularly comes,
We both pick her up from her mum.
She loves her wonderful niece . . .
As they sometimes watch the video, 'Grease'.

Works as a nurse most of the day . . .
When she arrives home, Chester wants to play,
Happily, he goes mad and wags his tail . . .
Whilst Gillian is feeling tired and very frail.

Goes and sees her friend Hills
Daily, as Hills ask, 'Do you want a refill?'
Drinking her tea as a guest . . .
Gillian you're the best!

Barry Ryan

AUNTIE GILLIAN

Auntie Gillian said . . .
we have no bread,
she looked in the larder,
and she tried to look harder.

So she popped to the shops,
there was a shelf at the top,
it was hard to reach,
and she slipped on a peach.
She banged her head,
so she had to go to bed.

Hannah Ryan (8)

P O E T S
PEOPLE'S ORDONNANCE EMANATING TENDERNESS; SINCERITY

(A piece of poetry with peace in mind)

P ortray your feelings in an easy form,
O rate and display the warmth within,
E voke the mind with which you were born,
T emptation; being the curse of sin,
R emember! Life can be so short and sweet,
Y our life, your ways, your years, to keep discreet.

I ndulge metaphorically in words of wisdom,
N urture and blend the scope of idiom.

M inutiae with mnemonic phraseology?
I nspiration, being the afflatus divine,
N oteworthy idyll's to euphoria sublime,
D elve in the depths, and create what you want to be.
   For poets are probity, and prefer peaceful ways,
   In transcribing their thoughts; for those future days.
   If! contentment could reign over this global ball,
   This world could offer much to all,
   For if each and everyone could share
   Life! would surely be; 'just and fair'!

William Johnson Lyth

CHECKOUT

Young Carol on the checkout counter
Full of first day smiles and silver eye line
Every new face
Is a charming embrace
To her time.

Young Carol on the checkout counter
Cheeks flush with hope and eyelids on fire
Learning the ways
On the halcyon days
Of desire.

Young Carol on the checkout counter
Tomorrow was just like today's repeat
Standing alone
In the sound of one's own
Heartbeat.

Fraser Hicks

AND ME?

And me, the little girl commands,
'Let me go too, I'll stay with you.'
Reluctantly I take the view
This must be what all brothers do,
Give in to such demands.

How wonderful, it's Saturday,
The cinema begins at nine,
'Don't worry Mum, we'll both be fine,
And yes her hand is clutching mine,
I'll watch her all the way!

Love grows with every passing year,
But whether they be wants or needs.
From rings to strings of coloured beads,
This is the hand from which she feeds,
The smile behind the tear.

Moya Hastings

REALISING AMBITION

Ambition often does a goal fast reaching seek
To satisfy a hopeful individual's desire for wealth or fame
Which often disappointing fails to obtain the highest peak
To reach the stars or in the headlines see one's name

Those urgent, strong desires by vivid fancy fired
To possess the many things this world can give
Want everything there is to be experienced or desired
Convince one's self this is the only way to live

Hoping to achieve these ends in one almighty leap
But then at rainbow's end no golden fortune find
So sadly trial and adversity make you weep
As hope is gone and all but dreams exist within the mind

Ambition does not always end this way
Heed warnings to look before you leap
Persevere and more slowly build to make worthy talents pay
Then one day the rewards of sowing you might reap

Ron Powell

SOFTNESS

I see the love you give to all
The sweet smile on your lips and in your eyes
I see how gentle your touch can be
The tenderness of your voice
I've seen all of these
As the years have gone by

The way you move so gracefully
As if you were a butterfly
When you come into a room
You bring with you a soft, warm glow
These feelings I have I cannot explain
As you lay beside me and the night goes by

Darling, you have never changed
I loved you from that very first day
Our love will never falter
So until the day comes when we must part
I will treasure those words you said
When we stood in front of God at the altar

George Potten

GOODNIGHT, MY NAN

So helpless, so powerless, I stood by your side,
Held your hand tight, while you slowly died.
I hated myself more, each, every day,
Being able to do nothing, while you slipped away.

Now looking back, those months seem like days,
Days that flew past me in one painful haze.
Now you are gone, and I miss you like mad,
Even happy memories to me now seem sad.

And memories are all I have now, to remember you,
Memories and your last words, 'I will always love you.'
Words that will stay with me now, be treasured in my heart,
I will always love you too, even when we're apart.

So, numb, I face reality, my new harsh life unfair,
Always longing to hear your voice, or see your smile of care.
I long and I wish, for one moment more,
One little more moment, when life's like before.

There's so many things I needed to say,
But now you have gone dear, I can't find a way.
I'm lost without you, completely alone,
I hurt, I've been shattered, my life has been thrown.

I face my cold future, without you by my side,
Without you to help me, without you to guide.
But no matter what, you'll always be here,
Here in my heart, where I hold you dear.

I asked why you left me,
Why did you die?
But I now see you,
Said goodnight, not goodbye.

Victoria Morley

SWANAGE PIER, SWANAGE, DORSET, ENGLAND

Let's go down to Swanage Pier,
Swanage Pier, Swanage Pier,
Let's go down to Swanage Pier,
To Swanage Pier, my dear.

Let's walk the planks in the salty air,
Salty air, salty air,
Let's walk the planks in the salty air,
To see what we can find there.

Sponsor a plank for Swanage Pier,
Swanage Pier, Swanage Pier,
Sponsor a plank for Swanage Pier,
For Swanage Pier, my dear.

Our names engraved on bronze plates dear,
Bronze plates dear, bronze plates dear,
Our names engraved on bronze plates dear,
Nailed into Swanage Pier.

So, let's take a trip to Swanage Pier,
Swanage Pier, Swanage Pier,
Let's take a trip to Swanage Pier,
And read my messages, my dear.

Don't care if you want to kill me my dear,
Kill me my dear, kill me my dear,
Don't care if you want to kill me my dear,
'Cause . . . it's an official fund-raising scheme, to save Swanage Pier.

Carol Ann Darling

GARDEN OF MANY FLOWERS

Did you ever see my garden, it has flowers of every kind,
There are beautiful flowers with variegated ivy called love

Flowers of honeysuckle called deepest affection of mind
Purples and pinks of kindness known to some as the foxglove

In my garden see roses of every colour and hue
Kisses by a lover's dew
Even bluebells a cup of human kindness

Bloom among the purple heather, rekindled love
Once lost renew, and stocks of many a
Father of the bride nonetheless

Did you ever see my garden, see the flower called a pauper's knee
And over there look an orchid's summertime

But in my garden the loveliest flower I see is the one
I know as eternal life, that is yours now
And one day will be mine.

Celia Meaker

SUMMER DAYS

The longer days are coming in sight,
Summer is near and the evenings stay light.
Puts a happy face on, when the sun shines through,
People are not so lonely, and the sky is more blue.

It is such a nice feeling just being outdoors,
The fresh air is so welcome and the day is yours.
People stop you and talk, when the weather is nice,
Always ready to listen and to give some advice.

The birds and the bees will be very busy soon,
The flowers and trees will be out in full bloom.
Colours are brighter in the clothes that we wear -
A sweet smelling aroma fills the air.

Summertime is a special time of the year,
We sit in the garden and enjoy a beer.
Sometimes till late we are still outside,
Watering the hanging baskets with such pride.

It is so nice in the morning to see a clear blue sky,
No dark clouds about, often means it will stay dry.
So lovely to go walking along the edge of the shore,
With the dog running in and out, barking for more.

The children building sandcastles in the sand,
What fun they have when Dad lends a hand.
In the sea, boats bob about, making a lovely sight,
The sun shining on them makes them look bright.

Summer is the months we look forward to most,
Everything has woken up, you feel warm as toast.
Make the best of this time, that's what I say -
Be thankful, and give thanks for this perfect day.

Carol Anne Crompton

CREATURE OF THE NIGHT

Eyes bright,
Skin taught,
Teeth sharp,
Breath short.

Rosemary Barter

LIGHT

The wind was cold as fear and the sea a gravestone grey
Colours dull and dreary, quelled the light of day
A shard of broken sunlight fell upon the twisted sea
And wavelets all a-glitter brought back the day to me

Ian Williams

THE LOST GARDENS OF HELIGAN

Tier upon tier: tree palms - like many fingered hands
Reach to the canopy - into the rich exuberance of green.
An orange profusion of azaleas
Tumbled about with garlands of white,
Lit from the heavens.
A warm intoxication of fragrance, gleam and vividness:
The flush of rhododendrons,
Heaped in bouquets of crimson –
Within, around, atop
The branches of this other Eden:
Reflect upon the mirror image, looking down;
Trees hang mysteriously beneath the tangled lily pads,
That hold their pastel blooms like delicate ceramics;
Dainty craft, floating above the azure depths,
As the sky saturates the centre
Of the still, green pool.

The woodland shade is splashed with sunshine.
A heaven of bluebells,
And the unfurling, lime-green freshness of the ferns
To cradle them;
Stars of wild garlic spike the air with pungency,
While birdsong echoes and exults within my soul.

For this lost Eden's re-emerging,
Its verdure nurtured lovingly:
Laboured at, sweated over,
To rediscover long forgotten beauty.
But this is not real Eden:
For in this daze of loveliness I know -
That garden was complete perfection, and - astonishingly,
So many more times ravishing than this!

Jane Clay

BEDTIME PRAYER

Before I close my eyes tonight,
One thing I ask of You,
Please don't make me wake in fright
From nightmares, weird dreams too,
Nor give me dreams of sadness
Lest I wake up feeling blue.

Instead, like babies let me sleep,
So peaceful and so sound,
So rapturous, and oh so deep
With calmness all around,
No dreams of fear or madness
That will leave me lost - not found.

I want to wake refreshed and bright
To get me through the day,
And once more sleep right through the night
To help me on my way,
Sweet dreams that make me feel so good
Is all that I do pray (for!)

Philippa Howard

THAT FUNNY CAT

I woke up one morning to see a funny sight,
I looked out of my window to the morning light.
And suspended over there, in the air,
Was a furry flying cat,
Fancy that.
But there was more to adore,
That cat had wings,
Of all the silly things.
These dark black wings were made of fur,
Not only that, but you could hear a purr.
A purr under the fur from that of an engine,
A little metal engine that kept those wingies beatin'.
And, oh did I hope
That it had a letter from the Pope.
Did it? Nope.
It just flew with the morning dew,
Outside my window, oh I'll never know.
But then it went,
And away it flew.
A flying cat I wish I knew.
But not that cat wanted to know me
Just came to laugh at me, hee hee.
Off it flew into a tree,
Now it was me
Who went hee hee.
Fancy that,
It's a dead cat.

Sebastian Bird

GLOUCESTER CITY

Gloucester, a cathedral city not a town
Where Lady Jane once claimed her crown
The Romans traded from within the gates
And still today we can see their many traits

Sunday schools were founded by Robert Raikes
Bishop Hooper and Heretics burnt at the stakes
The old tailor sewed till he had no more twist
Then mice took over from his weary wrist

Whittle gave us jet engines to aid World War II
And from Brockworth airfield the Javelin first flew
We gave Cotton motorbikes and Moreland matches
And locals still net spring Elvers in furtive catches

When redevelopment plans soon come to fruition
On this ancient city we hope to be in a position
To trade on our history and show once again
We are worthy of a visit by road, river or train

Jeannie Ashplant

LOST

I look up above, to a darkening sky
Spirit of Heaven, tell me why
What's the story? Why am I here?
It's bringing me down, I shed a tear

Before this day I was so sure
In the now dead past, I knew of a cure
Love and hope, kept me strong
So tell me spirit, what have I done wrong?

Rain washes, blends with my crying
Sea of tears in which I am dying
Falling to my knees, I curse the light
Sorrows beckon into the night

The past in mind needs a fix
The spirit watching, offer no tricks
I beg to it, change my fate
It shakes its head, it's too late

Robert Townsend

WALKING HOME

Walking home late at night
You're all alone, there is no light
A distant noise, a large dog's bark
You strain your eyes, it is too dark
Things start playing on your mind
Someone coming up behind
A lump in your throat like a ball
You're really scared, you want to call
A hoot a whistle, another sound
You're so afraid, you spin around
If you could see you wouldn't care
Squint to see there's no one there
Another noise up in a tree
Just too dark for you to see
Keep walking now, look straight ahead
All you want is your warm bed
Faster now you up the pace
You've just felt rain upon your face
Quickly now, you have to dart
You feel the pounding of your heart
You're in a panic, you start to run
This walking home for you's no fun
In front a glimmer of light appears
No more fighting back the tears
There's no more need for you to rush
No one hiding behind that bush
Your breath is short, your heart is pumping
You feel tired, your head is thumping
No more worry, your house you reach
The curfew you no more will breach.

Neil Warren

THE SLIMMED DOWN 'LITTLE RED RADISH'

Jimmy Whitaker has gone to town,
    His body bulk to slim right down,
Now after dieting, and much exercise too,
    The training instructor he set out to woo,
By showing intention weight-loss to achieve,
    With the fat disappearing, we now all believe.

He's now taken over, the No 1 Man,
    With set firm intention to keep to his plan,
An example to others, he now captains the team,
    Becoming more youthful, and looking all lean;
With his weight dropping off, he looks very good,
    More like his old self, no more than he should.

Adjustment in sizes he needs now observe,
    Like wearing old suits with his usual verve,
His neck and waistline have just melted away,
    Should he shrink anymore, he may rue the day;
As he's feeling much better than ever before,
    His reduced body size he need never deplore.

And for grim resolution in meeting regime,
    Warm praises we offer for keeping to time,
To show our approval, sponsorship we donate,
    For to Jimmy's great effort we all now relate;
So an end to the slimming, and also the jest,
    Or once in the office, he'll not fit in his desk.

Just remember to stay off the champagne, Jimmy!

Edward James Williams - A Bystander Poet

CHARDONNAY FLOWS

Chardonnay flows
Interspersed by laughter
Eyes smile
Candles flicker
Lives illuminated for awhile
And the eyes smile wider

Chardonnay flows
Lips touch briefly
Mouths explore in liberation
Caressing freely
Giving way to passion
Frantic hands remove lingerie

Chardonnay flows
Candlelit nakedness
Echoes of silence
Broken by breathlessness
Without moral defence
A stranger's sweet caress

Chardonnay flows
Fervent emotion
Naked bodies entwine
Loveless, passionate union
Intellectual decline
Fraudulent emotion

Chardonnay empty
Bodies again . . . adorned
Conversation falters
Laughter scorned
Relationship alters

And the taxi is called . . .

Steven J Smith

A Spring Night

Above, the moon,
an island in the indigo sea
lapping its shores.

At my back,
rough farmhouse stone
and the buzzing, oil-rich breath of the boiler.

In the orchard opposite,
rows of black trees, their branches
like umbrellas upturned by a sudden gust of wind.

Across the garden,
the chuckle and slow, steady beat of a little owl,
and the rhythmic chomping of the horses in the field beyond.

Beneath the hedge,
clumps of snowdrops and a solitary daffodil
elude the pattern of darkness.

A breeze,
passing lightly over my face,
seals the enchantment.

Caroline Smith

So Welcome!

The sun caresses the ground like a long awaited friend
After the misery of winter that seemed to have no end
The birds sing with joy for they too have longed for the sun
Flowers bloom in a bright array for they know summer has begun
The air glows softly, so warm and so clear
There is a feeling of much happiness for summertime is here

Sally-Anne Hardie

THE LOVER'S DREAM

We met on a bench in a park I thought it was love at first sight,
We started talking,
And had a lot in common,
I am glad I met you,
We walked around the park and then walked on towards my house,
He said I live down here,
I thought, *great, he lives so close I could see him all the time,*
I said we will meet up tomorrow,
My heart jumped a beat when he went to kiss me,
But instead he pulled me closer to him,
Then he kissed me,
Then I said I had to go but he wouldn't let me go,
My heart raced as though I was being shot,
But no it was just my alarm clock.

Emma Chapman

DON'T STAND AND STARE

Don't look at me and stand and stare
This is still me without my hair
Do you think that I like to be like this?
I can assure you sincerely, it's not my wish
To live my life my hair had to go
Are you aware how it pains me so?
I had no choice, the choice wasn't there
So please walk by, don't stand and stare
Don't you pull faces or make remarks
Bring your sense of humour, make me laugh
No one queries a man who's bald
So why does a woman need hair to be 'cool'?
Meanwhile a hat will suffice my need
Or a few pretty scarves to hide the deed
Hair shapes our faces, it's supposed to be there
So because I'm different don't stand and stare
I'm trying to accept it, I feel I've had my fair share
But to fight this cancer I had to lose my hair
It won't be too long and it will grow back
Then I won't have to wear my hats
Until that day comes show me love and care
As it's not a nice thing to stand and stare

Margaret Ward

CONFLICT OF EMOTION

I love you for the way you make me feel
I hate you for the way you make me ill
I need you but can't stand to see you
I wish I could tear myself in two
One to please myself the other to be with you
I don't know why I feel like this
I just know that it is true
Love you or leave you
I don't know what to do
This is a confusing situation
I'm in a conflict of emotion
And you think I'm playing a game
But you don't see my pain
And it's a shame
As you might understand
That I'm more than just one man
I am Mr Hyde
You may find that one day you'll decide
To leave me and then you'll see
I'm no good for you and you can do better
So goodbye my sweet, this is your Dear John letter

M A Beckett

ALONE

She sits alone, quiet and frail,
The room is dark, the air is stale.
Her only view of the world outside
Is through a window, five feet wide.
People pass by with urgent pace,
No one notices her fragile face.
Day after day sitting in her chair,
With outward glance and woeful stare.

Visitors have now become so very few,
Just meals on wheels with pies and stews.
A nurse periodically calls,
To check for slips, trips and falls.
No more for her the daily chores,
Her worries now are of pressure sores.
You'd think with sitting down all day,
The aches and pains would go away.

They say it's part of growing old,
How you always seem to feel so cold.
Even on a summer's day,
Those body shivers won't go away.
She can't even snuggle down in bed,
It's easier to sleep in the chair instead.
Life is so miserable, she's had enough,
When you're eighty-six, you're not so tough.

Of course it wasn't always this bleak,
She once was pretty, young and chic.
Sadly, her marriage years were only four,
Cut short when her husband never returned from the war.
Oh sure, she could have married again,
But the only man she wanted, was her Glen.
That day in church when she promised her heart,
It was with hope, they would never part.

So a life, she chose on her own,
No partner, no family, just her alone.
For a love so strong, that inside has stayed,
Was it worth the sacrifices that she made?
Sure another love would have been fun,
With perhaps a daughter or a son.
With so much time to reflect, is she bitter?
No, she just wishes she was fitter.

Robert Humphrey

SCRUMPING

Along the track run five faithful friends
Three in front, two lagging behind
The last two, deaf and partially blind
Determined to join in the fun

They know where they're going
They know what to do
Keep your head down
Keep out of view

Turn into the orchard - made it at last
Panting hard they've reached their goal
The pears look tempting, within easy reach
Of the five waiting mouths beneath

They've eaten their fill - their stomachs are full
And they're ready for their journey home
Their dinners await - mustn't be late
They think hard as they trot along

An apple a day keeps the doctor away
From our master's door, so they say
Perhaps the pears we have scrumped
Will keep away from *our* door
The scourge of all pets
The much-dreaded vets
Think the dogs as they make their way home!

Patricia Mackenzie

KNEELING

Kneeling
Quietness gathers,
Early morning
Illumines chapel,
Whisper of re-creation
Where myself pours out
Near tree golden
With a king's body.
Solitude brings special peace,
Death is dark country
You journey as souls seek
To cling as frail leaves
On tree threatened by dark winter.
You are king inhabiting my faltering praise,
You are near, silence becomes you
Pouring water from your wounded side
Here where nothing draws to itself
Like holy silence.

George Coombs

TO THE SUFFERING IN AFRICA

Their smile is as big as them,
Dancing teeth set in a grin.
Canoeing from cheek to cheek,
Currents of spittle froth as you speak.

Poised upon a lollipop head,
Breadstick neck,
The living dead.

Bones that barely hold your frame,
Skin transparent as a windowpane.
Rattling gurgles of shallow breath,
Wrack your riddled body,
And still your spittled smile shines deep,
Amidst the images of uneasy sleep.

Little children of the bush,
Crumbling back into the ochre sands,
Taking with you the disease of our land.

Katherine Corson

For The Moment

Yesterday I was hoping
Today I am regretting

Yesterday I was praying for salvation
Today I am praying for forgiveness

Yesterday I was longing for change
Today I am still waiting

Yesterday I was waiting for today
Today I am missing yesterday

Yesterday I thought my dreams would come true today
Today I realised I forgot to build them yesterday

Yesterday I was living for today
Today I live in yesterday

Yesterday has been and gone
Today though need not be another yesterday

Mark Anthony Games

COUNTRY LIFE

Mother's nails are thick with grime
And we all help out with the pigs
When she lowers herself to the chair
A sigh escapes from her lips
'A job well done,' she says with closed eyes
Too hard for you, my sad heart cries.

Her hair is wind blown, her cheeks afire
She smiles at concern
And lingers for a time
Self indulgence a rarity here.

Can we rest awhile? I ask
Something to eat and maybe a bath?
She smiles, shrugs
Eases out of the chair and walks to the stove
Where vegetables bubble to make a thick stew
'We will not starve,' she says
'The best of the land for you.'

I press my cheek to her hand
Feel roughness where all should be smooth
My beautiful mother so battered and worn
The life that she chose
Not to which I was born.

I was born within the sound of bow bells
Red buses and trams and trains
Lilies of the valley spread round the yard
Obscuring the smell of the drains.

So now we live in the country
With tractors and lorries and trees
But I yearn for the old days long ago
When there was space to do what I please.

J Williams

THE WEST PIER

Walking on the pier with Grandma
In the chafing wind,
Gloves on, cape well-buttoned,
Gaiters pinching,
I clutch a sixpenny wooden boat,
Then drop it.
It gets stuck in the woodwork.
That was nineteen twenty-seven.

The theatre looms, a glassy presence.
Strange machines line up,
With secret faces.
'Wait until you're older.'

At the end, where the fishermen
Spread bags and bait which wriggles,
Wooden stages, iron stanchions.
Oh, the sea is frightening
Toiling green and white below.
'I remember,' says Mother
'The night there was a storm
And the old Chain Pier was washed away.'

Now proud successor, facing your fate,
Rusted, battered and bedevilled,
Stay in our memories for generations,

Or maybe rise again?

Irene Snatt

COCKNEY RHYMING SLANG

Harry boy was Boracic Lint - he hadn't any loot.
He went to town to look for work in his only whistle and flute.
He washed his brass bands, shaved his boat race and combed
                                                        his Barnet Fair,
He took a tram to London Town, to seek his fortune there.
His dicky dirt was clean and pressed, his daisy roots were dapper,
His two mince pies were shining bright and a titfa was on his napper.
What a bit of luck, he thought, that he had no trouble and strife;
Only himself to worry about, so not such a bad old life.
And there it was, this big posh caff so he straightened his old blue fly,
Walked boldly in and asked for gaffer and told him that he would try
To be a dab hand at serving bangers and cups of Rosie Lee
Or anything else that he was ordered - a good waiter he could be.
Gaffer gave him the once over and filled him full of cheer
When he said that he would take him on and bought him
                                                        a large pig's ear.
It tasted good in his north and south and down his Derby kel.
He wouldn't have to walk the plank. He was really doing well.
And striding home, his plates felt great; he could have walked 'em off.
His tipped his titfa, brushed his tash and felt just like a toff.
Now the old Cain and Able would hold some decent grub
And he could have hot water in the old rub-a-dub.
No longer would he be boracic, no longer would he be a Jonah,
He'd be a regular Don Juan and find himself a Donah.
So life took a turn for Harry boy, a turn just for the best;
Good grub, pig's ear and snout in his hand from the ride he took -
                                                            up West!

Stella Haynes

THE LIGHTHOUSE

Grey rocks tumbling towards the sea
Seagulls soaring overhead
A lighthouse painted black and white
Rising towards the sky
Circular tower lost in a cloud
A flashing light just glimpsed
Aimed at sailors out at sea
Filled with wonder at the sight
Free as the gulls swooping by
Children clamber over rocks
Clear voices carry on the wind
'Look here is a wreck
Washed up on shore
A man lying over there
Was he shipwrecked do you think?'
A barrel floats nearby
Bottled wedged between the stones
'There must be treasure galore
Could this be whisky in the case?
Or a cache of golden coins
Maybe gunpowder from the war'
'Mum! Look what we have found'
'Leave that rubbish and come for tea'

Maureen Ashing

THE GOOD OLD DAYS!

Hailsham to Eastbourne, we used to go by rail,
But railway line is now a walk and cycle trail.
So Hailsham to Eastbourne, we have to go by bus;
Morning or afternoon that's OK - no fuss.
But evening for plays or shows we're really out of luck;
For bus timetable ends at 7pm and then, you're stuck!

Dorothy M Parker

MY DAY OFF

If anyone should ask you
How I spent my day,
Please tell them quietly
All I did was play!

I sat outside for breakfast
With the sunshine coming through,
The birds all singing round me
While I decided what to do.

Coffee by the tele
Watching half-an-hour of 'Friends'
Thinking how sad I'll be
When the series ends.

Cycle into Bournemouth
Chance meetings on the prom
Time for another coffee
Where shall we get that from?

Sit outside the Oceanarium
Coffee cup in hand
Sandals off, trousers rolled up
Toes wriggling in the sand.

Do a spot of shopping
New jacket and some shorts
Then back home to show off
Everything I've bought.

Now my day is over
Everyone is home
Cooking, homework, tidying up
Thank God my day's my own!

Rowena

UNTITLED

Winter by the sea is fun
One would not think it so
But under the rocks, and in the sun,
It's the South of France, you know.

Even when the wind is high
Providing it is in the north
We do not pause to reason why
But heads down, we sally forth!

The coastline stretching to Beachy Head
With not a soul in sight
Only the gulls with bits of bread
Winging their way in flight.

At the local market once a week
Our fruit and vegetables we buy
And round the stalls with others we seek
Some bargains - 'How cheap!' we cry.

The cattle, their faces drawn and cold
Wait for the farmer's call
The sheep are trying to look very bold
Herded against the wall.

The auctioneer, wanting the day's work done
Hurries his bids along
The farmers shaking their fists in fun
Bids him, 'Bang the gong!'

We have our lunch in The Homely Maid
An old fashioned inn well known
After a warm and our bill paid
We head the car for home.

Ruth King

Cardboard City

In back streets dark, cold and wet
Forgotten figures in corners slept
Ragged figures of human debris
Regrets and rats for company

Cardboard City, land of the lost
Afraid of the living, in fear of the frost
Surviving on wits, a day at a time
Circumstance their only crime.

If fate decreed that they should die
In passing without a single cry
Alone for company only fear
Who alone would shed a tear

There by fate, and not by choice
Souls in torment, with common voice
Drunks and addicts so absurd
Vanish daily, their pleas unheard

So spare a thought, as you sit to dine
Gulp your beer or drink your wine
Things taken for granted, as we often do
But for the grace of God, it could be you!

Graham Jones

CAPTURE THE IMAGINATION

Imagine a world with no imagination;
what would it be like not to dream?
Think what we'd be like without beliefs,
what if things were what they seemed?

There'd be no such thing as religion, no dolls that speak or fairy dust,
No wizards to fight the witches and no Peter Pan to rescue us.
All the heavens would be a hell, black and white would be the same,
Life would be one big bore; no one would have a goal or aim.

With imagination visit far off lands; take yourself way above the sky,
Dream you were king and ruled the land, or be able to say,
'The world is mine.'
You could be a singer with adoring fans, or ride on a great white shark,
You could win over all your fears, and be able to sleep in the dark.

Even if you're a grandmother, you can still have child beliefs,
Just take a while and sit down still; imagine being a cat or a leaf.
If you're feeling down or alone, just get stuck into a book;
It will take you to far off planets; so get one out and take a look.

You know the saying, *as young as you feel*; stay a child
as long as you must,
Your outside doesn't come in at all, but in your heart
stay sparkling - don't rust.
So whenever you feel you are growing too old,
too sensible, careful or true,
Don't even think about the outside; look deep down
- what's the real you?

So dream every day, dream every night, use your imagination with ease,
Share your beliefs with everyone, and keep the world at peace.

Amy Stamp (14)

STRAWBERRY SNOW

Along Rochester's Northgate, up to the cathedral,
There stands a row of flowering cherry trees.
In spring they are attired in tutus of rosy pink
And they become a Mecca for the bees.
In summer they are green, giving shelter from the sun,
Shading the quaint tea shop selling ice creams,
For panting dogs and owners, a respite from the heat,
And schoolboys, as they dream their summer dreams.
In autumn the leaves turn subtly, vivid gold and russet,
Before the wind brings them to the ground.
They pile in crunchy mounds along the cobbled path,
Children rustle through them, tossing them around.
Winter brings frost and snow, painting branches white
And in the gloom the trees stand stark and bare,
Underneath the surface changes are taking place,
Nature's cycle of life is working there.
Suddenly it's spring again, with sunny days so fair,
Those frothy blossoms once more deck the trees.
After reaching the pinnacle of their spectacular short stay
They become a strawberry snowdrift, on the balmy breeze.

Patricia Adele Draper

THOUGHTS ON KENT

To wander down a Kentish lane in spring
And see the apples ripen on the bough
To hear the cuckoos call across the fields
A welcome to the season with us now
This, all I ask, though but a simple plea
Is one that brings such happiness to me.

To sit beneath the tree in summer's sun
And feel the warming breeze upon my face
To watch the gentle ripples on the stream
And marvel at this peaceful, perfect place
This, all I seek, to make my heart rejoice
And still that inner quiet, but troubled, voice.

To kick the autumn leaves in dancing swirls
And wonder at the trees bare-limbed once more
To smell the smoke of far-off timber fires
And see the farmer standing at his door
This, all I need, to comfort rainswept days
As, to the warmth of home, I turn my gaze.

To hunch my shoulders 'gainst the winter's squall
And pull my collar tight to stop the chill
To scrape the mud from boots left at the door
From trudging homeward up that final hill
This, all I want, my tiny piece of Kent
In which my lifelong years are gladly spent.

Michael D Swift

SECOND CHANCES

If you're given a chance,
Then take it.
Prove what you can do.
Make a difference,
Change the world.
Don't waste it like a fool.

If you're given a chance,
Realise it.
Use it to go far.
Make an effort,
Reach your goals.
Discover who you are.

If you're given a chance,
Don't lose it.
Expecting to get more.
Chances are rare.
Chances are gifts.
Second chances aren't for sure.

Leah O'Connor

DUNGENESS

There's no place quite like Dungeness,
It has a fascinating lure;
That never-ending wind's caress
Ensures the air is clear and pure;
It is a bleak and lonely place
Of shingled waste and stony space.

Offshore in sixteen-fifty-two,
The Dutchman, Marten Tromp trounced Blake
And for the moment did subdue
The English, leaving in his wake
Three sunken ships. He claimed the day,
And went triumphant on his way.

And many ships have come to grief
Upon this bleak peninsular,
Their wreckage cast upon the reef
Of shingle - cargo, cask and spar
And bodies too, despite the light,
Upon the point, which shines so bright.

Bleak Dungeness, a world apart,
Inhabited by fishermen
Of sturdy build and mighty heart.
Men always ready, as and when,
To man the lifeboat, risk their all,
To answer each disaster call.

A power station now looms large
Upon the west and windward shore.
Dire threat of nuclear discharge
Is something no one can ignore.
Such fears the changing times may thwart,
The station's forecast life is short.

May Dungeness return to be
That shingled wilderness of old,
A place where wild birds may roam free,
A haven of strong winds and cold.
May visitors be keen, but few,
Take preservation as their cue.

Jax Burgess

HOME AT LAST

I love to roam these old familiar lanes,
deep within the Kentish countryside.
And see, within the distance, lambs, newborn,
and riders on their ponies, side by side.
Sweet violets growing freely at my feet,
their perfume wafting through the morning air.
the hazy sunshine and the old ewe's bleat,
the lazy cattle, grazing, stop to stare.
And now, as I look westward, I can see
a lovely little cottage, all oak-beamed;
that well-loved figure, standing at the door,
oft, of this precious moment I have dreamed.
And so, at last, (my childhood long since flown),
I run toward this haven of my past,
on footsteps swifter than I've ever known
and cry aloud with gladness, 'Home at last!'

June Edridge

UNTITLED

The puppet man who pulls the strings
to make us do god-awful things,
sits in His big chair and grins
as He forgives us, for His sins.

P W Corbett

DOWN IN THE VALLEY

My delight and inspiration,
My paradise sublime,
Is no esoteric destination
In some sweet exotic clime.
It's of no particular beauty,
Though its life is sometimes wild.
To go may seem a duty
Hope torn and pride defiled
It is not a national treasure,
Although some may think it so,
But it gives a lot of pleasure
To aficionados in the know.
Afternoons of thrills and heartaches,
Ups and downs, and highs and lows.
Sweat and toil, and skill and smart breaks,
Kicks and rushes, spills and throws.
Ghosts of now forgotten heroes
Sway across the hallowed ground,
Prima donnas and proud primeros
In old memories are found.
It's a special happy valley
Where Charlton make their home,
A spot where you can dally
Just a stone's throw from the Dome.
A cathedral of romances
Where the Valiants make their name,
Where the atmosphere enhances
The noble football game.

Jack Scrafton

DARE

Don't define yourself by your job.
You and me we both have to work.

I don't care where you went to school,
which university or hall,
just if you learned to feel alive.

I don't need to know your income
gross or net, for the things I need
from you can't be bought anywhere.

Fancy dining won't impress me,
what is it that you hunger for?

Don't speak to me of politics
unless it drives your soul.

That flashy label or the cut
of your suit will not persuade me.
Show me the ugliness in you.

Don't try turning me to your faith
instead, make me believe in you.

Don't tell me of your Porsche owners' club,
but tell me of your failures.

Don't tell me where you went today
instead show me where your mind goes
when caution and reason have left.

And I am not interested
in how great people think you are,
but in whether you would risk it all.

C S Rowland

LADDER OF LIFE

I was a daughter, so happy and free,
Two sisters made me the youngest of three.
Surrounded by love was such a pleasure,
Childhood memories, that I still treasure.

Then I grew up and became a wife,
But still it continued, my happy life.
Making a home where we both could live,
Learning to love and how to forgive.

Then, when a mother I became,
Life was never quite the same.
Busy home full of love and laughter,
I wondered what would come thereafter.

Now I'm called either Granny or Nan,
And I love to help whenever I can.
O the love, joys and laughter given by my family,
How lucky I am that I was born me.

Lyn Budd

My Valentine

If you were my valentine
I'd be in seventh heaven
I hope I'm not too old
Not too decrepit
Mature love
Is so exciting
Like mature burgundy
Colour of the darkest rose
You colour my life
In red, yellow and gold
In a rainbow of colour
So my love
Please be my valentine
And let us travel together
On that rainbow of love
If you would be my valentine.

Patricia Turner

MAKE A STAND

Like the weep of the willow
we cry silent tears,
like the old oak tree
we will stay here for years.

We will bend with the wind
as far as we dare
and bask in the sun
when the rain's soaked our hair.

The want of the green
to colour our land
should be all the reason
we need, make a stand.

Vicki Billinghurst

THE EVACUEE

You are going away
to catch a train
4 years old, label on coat
teddy under arm
crying parents
screaming children

You are going away
to catch a train
strange place
strange people.
Where's my mum?
Where's my dad?

Who is the lady
that chose me
and took me from the train?
I miss my mum
I miss my dad
crying for home
the things I had known
the day they took me away
on a train.
The tears still flow
remembering that day
they took me away
on a train.

Doreen Simson

ONE STEP FORWARD AND TWO STEPS BACK

One step forward and two steps back,
Try to keep my mind on track,
Think about things, again and again,
All this helps to shut out the pain,
I know I am taking one step forward and two steps back,
Making no progress, staying in one place,
Every day is so hard to face,
Our time together was just divine,
And now my love, we are out of time,
So I will take one step forward and two steps back,
And bide my time alone,
Keep on smiling, our seeds are sown, darling I should never moan,
Try to keep my mind on track,
Cherish my memories, love you more, and just keep moving along,
By taking one step forward and two steps back . . .

Caroline Charman

So Close But Far

Behold the haste, the days end
Of two silent lovers, suspend
Without publicity and lies

Spilled time results, their indecision
Another party controls their bodies
But not their thoughts and eyes

To believe a connection
Between two can exist
Devoid of conversation and openness

Remarks of human instinct
Dreams turn to life
Still they wait

A chance to touch, smell, cuddle and cry
They have to trust their fate
All lonely souls must bide.

B Manhire

AUTUMN ACORNS

There's an ancient knurled oak,
    Its limbs are thick,
Swollen with the gout of age.
    They spread, they intertwine
Like gymnasts, some above,
    And some below, in acrobatic show.
They sway and court the wind
    That gives them grace,
And music rustles in their swing.
    Feather-light, bright coloured wings
Flutter through them, never still.

Ancient knurled oak,
    Thy trunk defeats the ravages of time:
Your smooth brown acorns, autumn fruit,
    Will ever gleam like polished ovals
On the windswept dry-leafed ground.

Connie Laurent

Darren

He walks alone
Through the shadows of the night,
Knowing what he's doing,
Being gone by light,

A single tear
Spread down his face,
That marks the memory
And takes its place,

A disastrous life
That's full of shame,
Will be ended soon
When he clears his name.

His daughter will hurt,
His son and wife will cry,
As he ends his life
With no reason why

As the sorrowful strangers
On the edge of life,
He stops to think
To comfort his wife

'Don't worry my dear
for all will be well,
just think of me in Heaven,
and think not of Hell.'

Vicky Jones

TRAINING ANTICS

We were all marching back to tea
It had been raining hard
Our order was, 'Half right, round the wet.'
In case we were off guard.

Another day we had our phones
And passed the message on
Until Mary said, 'What's for tea?'
The sergeant said, 'It's done.'

'Stop thinking about your stomach
Every time we stop.'
But Mary loved all her rations
Ate and drank the last drop.

She was slim and easy going
Took life much like a game
One night a doodlebug cut out
We dived out of its claim

Once going home in fog and frost
We hardly knew our way
We caught a bus, and travelled on
It took nearly all day.

Edith Buckeridge

THE UNFORTUNATE SLIP UP

Cedric the *class know it all* dorky geek
shuffled about as though wanting a leak.
The cheeks of his bum kept moving apart
as though he was going to let out a fart.
His shoulders were hunched and his knuckles were white
but nobody dared to ask, 'Are you alright?'
Sitting in silence the class read their book
with only the brave daring to look
to see what young Cedric was going to do.
Would he *dare* to admit that he needed the loo?
His face was all red, his eyes starting to close
a big blob of snot hanging out of his nose.
The teacher, oblivious to Cedric's hot flush
turned on the tap to wash her paintbrush.
The sound of the water was too much to bear
when all of a sudden from out of nowhere
a puddle appeared by Cedric's right shoe
closely followed by a little brown poo.
The teacher walked back to her desk unaware
of the puddle and poo next to Cedric's chair.
She put down her foot only to find
the next thing she knew she was on her behind.
Her legs in the air, her skirt round her ears
the whole class erupted with whoops and with cheers.
Poor Cedric was mortified, glued to the floor
while the rest of the class legged it out of the door.
The next day they acted like nothing was wrong
but the couldn't escape from a terrible pong!

Wendy Orlando

THE OFFICE BOY

Jonathan works in our office of law,
He wants to study to become a big bore,
Although he's a nut we find him disarming,
With sentences like 'How perfectly charming.'
He stands 9 feet ten with a head like a book
He has a nose like a curtain rail hook,
His hair is right down to his knees would you know.
His chatter is like an incessant flow.
His tummy hangs over the top of his trousers,
Held up by a belt made out of girls' blouses,
He wears a big grin that forever is spreading,
It stretches from Tooting and ends up in Reading.
To get a true picture of what he is like,
He travels to work on a three-wheeled bike,
And it's really enough to give you the traumas,
When he stands in the doorway in pink flannel warmers,
But now that my story is now nearly done,
I tell you it all was made up just in fun.
For Jonathan really isn't this bad
Believe me he's really a very nice lad.

E M Housman

SLOW DECLINE

I live in London - it is no fun.
People are warming to the sound of the gun,
The knife is becoming old hat, seems to me
I'm leaving London for the sound of the sea.
Lawless streets, kids on the make
Whose house next do they decide to break?
Do what they like - get no slap
No respect, when on crack.
No discipline, no rules, no clout from the cop
I now wonder if and when it's going to stop.
Adults are nothing, it's the kids that rule,
Shame the kids don't appreciate school.
Shame their brains are wasting away
Smoking pot and crack all day.
Hooded up they go a-walking
Down the alleyways they go a-stalking.
Easy prey they're looking for,
Walk along - what door? What door?
Little old lady now fights for her life,
Gun-toting kids - yeah, they're rife!

Gillian Maynard

LUST

I have found her now!
Nothing left to do but wait.
What price destiny?
Chance goes hand in hand with fate.

I had searched for years,
For what, I never knew,
Then I realised
It was not a what, but who?

Strange how one can tell.
One meeting such as this,
And my heart was hers.
She - my catharsis.

She is so beautiful.
Skin with the blush of youth,
Eyes clear innocence,
Lips that know only truth.

I must make her mine.
But how with one so young?
For age can cause divides.
Must my love remain unsung?

Every day I see her,
But restrain myself I must.
To her I am but nothing,
But my love now turns to lust!

Today I touched her!
Oh God! Ecstatic bliss!
Skin so smooth - so warm!
Breath sweet as a lover's kiss!

Have her now I will!
Yes and soon! It must be soon!
And I will slake my lust,
Beneath a madman's moon.

Yes I know I'm mad!
For this sinful curse of mine
Cannot be right I know.
I kneel at the Devil's shrine!

*   *   *   *   *   *

I have had my way!
It is over - now she cries,
All innocence lost
From her swollen tear-filled eyes.

See how she stares at me.
Does she perceive my shame?
Well, perhaps she does
But I would do it all again.

She knows I love her,
And our secret it must be.
To share with no one
Or all is lost for me.

She is not the same,
For where once happiness shone
There's but a dull façade.
Her love of life has gone.

What right have I
To play my adult tricks,
And so to blight the life
Of this lovely child of six?

Bob Crossley

DREAMING

Just close your eyes and imagine what might have been
when you were young.
The pageant queen. When you grew up the prince would come
and carry you off on his stallion.
Young men calling with blooms in arms, vying for your
virtuous charms.
Travelling far to distant climes, tropical sunshine, dusky smiles.
Then open your eyes and you will see, swollen ankles and
arthritic knees.
Dark bare trees and pouring rain, it's winter again.
Just for a while things were grand lying in a sunny land.
When life is hard and times are lean everyone can sit and dream.
So shut your eyes and come with me, I'm off again, I've drunk me tea!

Veronica E Terry

LAZY SEA

Gentle calm sea, seems to have tarried too long
For now it's hurrying, the waves have become strong
It whispered it's returning, with a hypnotic, serene wail
Yes, it tarried a while, while we played in its trail

Now white horses are galloping, gulls surf on their mane
To become quite motionless, time after time again
Lulling awhile, while shore life takes its turn
Then back on its journey, to distant shores to return

Susan E Roffey

MAY AND ME

Life on the home front was hard I know
Bombs and doodlebugs, and winter's snow.

Death and destruction was all around
Our house that day . . . was razed to the ground

Not a cup or a saucer was . . . recovered
And the voice saying . . . 'Don't stand and stare, move along Mother!'

No money or clothes, nowhere to stay
We were taken away . . . from Mum that day

'You'll like it,' Mum said, she promised to write
'Don't cry or you'll look a proper sight!'

To live with strangers, me and May
Away from the war . . . into the country far, far away

On the platform I stood clutching May's hand
Longing for Dad . . . fighting in some foreign land

'Come on,' Mum said, 'it won't be for long,
I'll see you quite soon.' Oh how she was wrong

I never saw Dad . . . he was killed by some flack
Mum was killed in a factory . . . found dead by a pile of old sacks

Yes! Life on the home front was hard I know
Some have medals, for us, no memories of parents to show.

Sylvia Connor

FREEDOM

I want you to free your mind
So you can bob about,
From thought to thought.
Like a plastic duck
In a lover's bath.
Free to swim from
Idea to grand idea.
With no mundane daily ties.
Take just a few moments,
In every lacklustre day
To ponder the absurd,
To travel to the non-existent,
To take the hand of every possibility,
To win on every level,
Not to compromise but expand.
To shove aside all,
If, buts and maybes.
And go sailing in the bliss,
Of a pure you Heaven.
The world will not alter,
While you are on your voyage
But the answers you were searching for
May be waiting.

Jan Cowper-Smith

A Scorned Soul

I will shed no more tears
For there is only room for laughter
I shall not forget your treachery
Now and ever after.

I laugh at how you write to me
As if life were still the same
But betrayal cannot be disguised
By any other name.

I jest at how you comprehend
That which you have done
But in honesty I can't believe
How twisted you've become.

Actions speak and victims weep
But I will not be fallen
Do not pretend it matters not
Your pride should not be swollen.

I'll write no more and close my lips
For my words are surely wasted
I hope that you are happy
In the bitter life you tasted.

Hannah Pay

MAKE THE MOVE!

Buying a house and perusing plans
Striving hard to pass exams
Betting on horses, running free
Praying for a fortune on the lottery
Sowing seeds to make new plants
Sowing the seeds for a lad in pants
Saying 'I love you' to someone nice
Being scared will not suffice
Little things that do make sense
Risking a little for recompense
Allowing the kids on a fairground ride
Showing your family that they own your pride
Enquiring for a loan to furnish a room
Playing safe before it ends in doom
Informing another that you they impress
Hoping for a lot, well more or less
Considering additions to the family
Hoping that the wife will it agree
Looking smart to apply for work
Putting on the style, then going berserk
Drinking pop and avoiding gin
Hoping it will improve the lot you're in
Counting blessings that come your way
Looking forward to the coming day
A little of what you fancy does some good
One understands if it is understood
Depending on a result with sweet returns
Spending within limits of what one earns
Grab hold of the reins before it be too late
With a little initiative one may not get by
Nothing will be achieved unless *you try!*

John L Wright

HANDWRITING - A LOST ART

Revealing
- beautiful and stylish.

Scribble
- that poor substitute
becoming a rare personal revelation
in this computer age.

Unwittingly,
- our emotions clearly expressed
when even a few words
are written by hand,
in times of stress.

Handwriting
- inspires many a poet's thoughts
in this personal art.
Putting pen to paper
can ignite remarkable response.

Margaret Ann Wheatley

NEW YEAR

You stand waiting for the famous countdown to begin,
And herald in a new year, one free of your old sin.
So much can happen and change in only one short year,
So many chances to win or lose what you hold dear.

But that year and all of its many chances are dead.
That is one thought that really must get into your head.
There is no way of going back, reclaiming the past,
As time will forever continue to race so fast.

One year dies, but as it does, so another is born,
One which is still capable of making you feel torn.
When you don't know what is the right way to act or feel,
Or even if what you think you are feeling is real.

From the decisions you have made and those you will make,
You will begin to see and discard all that is fake.
So take this new year and embrace all that it may hold.
Laugh, cry and love but never be afraid to be bold.

Becky Morris

A Little Time With Me

You never know who you're going to meet
When you're in love, love is sweet
I met you and a love did grow
Soon my love began to show
Now its roots are oh so deep
And in my heart, this love does keep
I have to love you from afar
But my love, it holds no bar
No matter what you say or do
My love just grows and grows so true
I sit here and I spend my time
Nurturing this love of mine
Although this love you don't return
This love is deep and it does burn
I hope God in his heart can see
To let you spend a little time with me
I will wait my whole life through
I will only *ever* want to be with you.

Suzy Verma

SHHHH!

Do realise, we're all asleep
Asleep or dead, our consciences
Be silent! You forget we bleed
For past killing, maiming, neighbours.

Alright, we would be speaking Dutch
German, Romanian, Swedish
Or would you perhaps prefer French?
What makes perfect, speaking English.

To properly prepare pronounce
They say you need to purse your lips
No frown or judging look askance
Instead, your stance the same to kiss.

Kissing cousins, whatever race
All fam'ly, relations with God
So let's forget the wars, solace
To heal: wounds forgotten, love, fond.

Gerasim

SEASONS OF LIFE

In springtime we are children, it does not last very long;
We grow and are told things, what's right and what's wrong.
We go to school to learn and play, we're full of hopes and dreams,
At the start of life's journey - well that's how it seems.

Then suddenly it's summer, we're nearly full grown;
It's time for us to go to work and learn to stand alone.
We start to build lives of our own, to learn of love and strife,
To find a future for ourselves to take us through our life.

In autumn we are middle-aged, our lives are all planned out;
We know what our tomorrows bring, our future has no doubt.
We have come to accept what life holds in store;
Our dreams are now reality, we do not ask for more.

And finally, it's winter when we are old and grey,
And look back on our memories of every golden day.
The pace of life is quieter now and at a slower rate;
But time seems to pass so quickly, it's the master of our fate.

To each and everyone of us the seasons of life will pass;
From springtime into winter, whatever creed or class.
And as we look back through all the years and remember when
                                                      we were young,
'Tis only now we realise the best is yet to come.

Beth

HERB WOMAN

She was a whiz with cloves and apple pies
Her dill cream fish dish
Satisfied every wish
She spun ruby jellies from raspberries.

She stitched lavender-filled pillows
With soft flowing white lace
Tender for the sore face
She hung bronze tansy high to repel flies.

She lined her sills with pots and baskets
Brewed basil potion
For ulcer gum lotion
She dreamed of a fine camomile lawn.

She strewed feathery-rich rosemary
Next to snaps of the dead
And roses for the wed
She gentled nursery rhyme marigolds.

She bubbled borage to give courage
To the nervous in need
Of solace or a good feed
She placed heart ease on her stone doorstep.

She wept when at last her husband left her
Hay fever ridden
To seek solace hidden
And mourned with forget-me-nots and rue.

Sarah Williams

SHADOW

As I stumbled down the alley,
It was as black as night,
Splash, sploosh with puddles shouted,
The wind howled between the creaking houses,
The shadows were almost like the cape of a man, hiding as I passed,
Whose breath gusted up behind me and made me shiver,
The sharp rain pitter-pattered on my shoulders,
As I reached my door,
The key clicked into the lock
The shadow pounced . . .

Liam Satchell (12)

WORDS ON LOVE

Hearken to me the very essence of my life,
I thank you for the joy
That in my heart and feeling you inspire,
With the substance of nature,
And the great spirit.

That forever fills these lands,
With the beauty immeasurable,
To the keen eye that observes deeply
And sees a miracle in all of life.

There is nothing without love,
Even wisdom would be nothing,
Were it not for the warmth in the breast
Towards all beings,
Beings who laugh in felicity,
And beings who suffer in great woe.

I hold to the principal of truth,
That love opens the eyes to the truth
And the truth is concrete,
For even in my adversities I love
And strive not to have.
Love is strong and builds upon itself,
For it must be practised
As the foundations of all life and the earth itself
Is found in love.

Tim Weeks

TEARS OF JOY

Tiny fingers, tiny toes
Beautiful blue eyes and a button nose
Masses and masses of shiny dark hair
Your very first cry like music in the air

Nine months of waiting to hold you here with me
Waiting so anxiously for your precious face to see
Somewhat like Daddy and somewhat like me
So proud to say 'us', not as two but now three

Never knowing a feeling of love like this could exist
So deep, so intense, for nothing more could I have wished
A whole new world to look forward to baby, now you're here
As I hold you in my arms and whisper in your ear
Hello my precious angel, my beautiful baby boy
This is me, I'm your mummy, as I weep my tears of joy.

Esta Taylor

CHURCHES! CRICKET AND CARNIVAL!

Somerset my county, I live in the County town
Taunton is the town I live in
Surrounded by hills all around.

I have a view from my window
The bedroom being best
Where I can see four churches
Oh I do like it here in the west.

There's Holy Trinity, St George's and St James
To name a few
But the one in our town centre, St Mary's
You must visit if ever you pass through.

We have a theatre named The Brewhouse
And of course for cricket, County Ground,
And a lovely park called Vivary
It's a thriving county town.

In August, the annual flower show
That is held in the park, year by year
There are beautiful flowers to look at
And bands; 'music to the ear'.

We have Carols by Candlelight
As well in the park
We have marathons and carnivals too
And very nice shops and farmers' market
And you can visit a pub or two!

It's central to live in the County town
You can soon get to the sea
Visit places like Minehead, Weston or Burnham,
Cheerio now and I might see thee?

Rachel Mary Mills

CHRISTMAS FOR US

Our stockings are put at the foot of the bed
Mummy kisses goodnight after prayers are said.
We are so excited, we cannot sleep,
Now it's dark, shall we take a peep -
To see if Santa has come to us yet?
I wonder what toys we both will get?
'I would like a dolly,' said Jane.
Joe said, 'I would like a toy aeroplane.'
It's daylight now, we can open our eyes.
Oh look Joe! What a lovely surprise.
There's my dolly all dressed in blue
An aeroplane Joe is there for you too.
Our stockings are full, there's an apple and pear.
Oh look, there's a chocolate teddy bear!
A bag of sweets, Maltesers too
I love Maltesers Joe, do you?
A pink sugar mouse, I'm sure we'll find
I think Santa Claus has been most kind.
To thank him a letter we must write
For coming to us on Christmas Night.
So many children he had to see
But he didn't forget Joe and me,
We are sure dear Santa you need a rest
So goodbye dear Santa and God Bless!

D R Webber

TOE THE LINE

Is your intention to pour his wine with exaggerated affection,
only to please?
Your subservience willingly accepted and no obvious
displeasure shown (For fear of retaliation perhaps?)
The delusion of bliss, lost with that first kiss.
Has cruel fate once again played the trickster?
Knowing you will concede the battle before it has even begun.
Do you feel rage or pity for yourself?
Can the rage command armies of strength to break down the
fortress of subjugation?
Or are you enslaved in the dungeon of self-pity, weeping for
the way out to reveal itself, when all the time you hold the key.
Do you look at others and envy their euphoria?
Knowing that you must settle for the boorish sovereign
whose territory is marked with your emotional scars?
Now is the hour to fulfil your potential, the certainty of birth
and death remain untouched
Knowing that, will you tolerate your life?
With confidence, search for your destiny; wage this war
upon yourself no more.
You are beautiful.

Michelle Cunningham

A CATECHISM

I went to visit my old gran.
A wedding guest I'd been
And so my gran asked me to tell
The things that I had seen.

She asked me many questions
About the wedding day,
And these were just the kind of things
My grandmother did say.

'What colours were the bridesmaids' frocks?
How did you like the bride's?
What were the flowers in her bouquet?'
And many more besides.

'The bridesmaids' dresses were of silk
Patterned in green and white.'
I said, 'As for the bride's own dress
For her, it was just right.

She carried flowers in her bouquet
Of many a different kind.
Red and white rosebuds were in those
Of the maids who walked behind.'

'Where did they go for their honeymoon -
Tell me, where they did go?'
My granny bade me. I replied
'They went to Westward Ho!'

'What did she wear to go away?'
My granny asked me then.
'Well,' I replied, 'I couldn't say
They went, I don't know when

After they'd had a disco, which
Did not appeal to me.
She hadn't changed, no, not a stitch,
When I went home to tea.'

And when I'd answered questions
On what I'd had to eat
And if they'd had a buffet, or
I'd sat upon a seat

My gran gave o'er her questioning
About the wedding day,
And having told her all I could
I slowly went away.

Jillian Mounter

Memory Garden

There's lady's fingers
That's for my mother,
Green thumbed and sowing
In improbable places:
Balconies in China,
Plant pots in Michigan,
Patios in Penang.

There's pineapples,
Planted by the chain-link fence,
To discourage burglars,
A blue-sword surprise for any
Creeping thief,
Venturing into my adolescence,
The prize I imagined them guarding
All the more illusory,
After the fall.

There's papayas,
A whole grove of these
Astarte-chested trees,
Shielding the kitchen
From catcalls of the village boys.

There's *lalang* or elephant grass,
Sharp as a knife and inescapable,
Letting blood if I was careless
And turned my back on the sharp points of
Small town life.

There's the red grass seed,
Flowering on the empty lot,
I gathered it in armfuls of feathery air,
Blowing away through the glass-louve red windows,
Great clumps of pink yearning -
To set down roots,
To cover the earth,
To be anonymous and simple
As the humble blade.

Pey Colborne

TELL ME?

Tell me
As we walk along the shore,
Crests sobbing on a gritty breast.
Did your love not die but fade
As the summer lark falls to rapacious autumn?
I broke a little each day,
Watching, waiting.
Knowing that your eyes had lost
That sweet tenderness that marked me as yours.
I smiled to friends
Glorious in summer, yet dreading winter
And as quiet snows sweeps over our bones
As goodbyes are said,
I watch the stars fall to dust.

Kyra Louise Reynolds

Is Earth Bursting?

Ozone hole gets bigger
Satellites blocking light
Question now is how soon
Is Earth going to blow?
Technology, is it helping
Or does it make one cry?
Fifty years surrendered
Maybe gone with speed.

M D Bedford

COMING HOME IN WINTER

Along the bank poplars stand in meadow gone river
their sky-edges coot colour all depth
lost in all scrudge
old time markers ripplewise into

fog a paste a pollock-on-valium apathy
getting the pores under the lashes beyond nose
bones damp papiermachéd
summer: a memory backdrop
a sprouting bean blotting paper

jammed flat in a jar for a kid
happy a stain end a cold jaundicy shoot
      a crescent moon. Flood plain is
      a moon fantasy pink
4pm sun gone down brief pre
sneeze feel moment only relief

The pretty a mirage in the desert of loss
a sump vortex of sadness
but even this more than the fullest Gulf
the sum total of baby pastel sunsets
love sweat bonding between palms
false promise of lust the not much

left to say hopeless empty dusk
that for all its mindinglessness eyefuls
is beaten hands down by this dead season

AnnMarie Eldon

THE HOLOCAUST

It was a day of reckoning,
A Hell unleashed on Jews,
The dogs of Hell come beckoning,
Our fate, we cannot choose.

I see the fear in their eyes,
As each second passed by.
The looks of the guards upon us
Just daring us to cry.

We're made to stand on the edge of a pit,
As the soil beneath us burns,
Stained with the blood of the innocent,
Each shot is fired in turns.

They fall until they crash
Upon the spent earth.
Mothers, children, workers
Lay spent from a prejudice birth.

The bodies continue to pile up
And the showers are the promised land.
Though my trek through the desert
Ends with nothing but black sand.

So as I stare into the empty pit
And pray for that lifting thought
I already know
That my fate has already been bought.

So with my last words I say
That not lost are my counterparts,
For below where their bodies lay
Heaven has freed their hearts.

Alex Edwards

FREEDOM

Freedom -
To walk along a river bank
Early in the morn
To see the heron rising
On widespread silent feathers;
The ducks and geese
Go noisily flapping -
The swans on squeaking wing.
The chaffinch and the robin
In orchards, gaily sing.

The tidal river moving
Between its wide spaced banks
Moving to the sea and that which lies beyond.
And with its seaward progresss
The sandbanks are revealed.
An early morning walker
Views this early morning scene
Added to the melee, singing church bells peal.
The dew still lies upon the grass
As swallows dive and wheel.

The smell of new mown grass
May blossom and cow parsley,
The sky a cloudless blue
Sun warm upon the walkers back
Freedom . . .
An English summer morning
Water lapping 'gainst the breakwater
With its subtle warning,
But all in all
Freedom - an English summer morning.

Yvonne Bulman-Peters

May Display

The wildly extravagant month of May
With its bewitching beauty and smells
Clothes the hedgerows in vibrant hues
And awakens the sleeping bluebells

Nature flaunts herself brazenly
In such dazzling array
Of green trees and gorgeous blossoms
It takes your breath away

Spring lambs leap happily
Birds sing all day
Can there be anything more glorious
Than the month of May.

Olive Homer

ODE TO A MAN WITH A MUSICAL GAIT

I know a bloke with creaky old shoes
When he walks
His feet they sing the Chaplin blues
A lil' bit quirky
Like Chaplin's crooked stick
If he gets up ahead
I'm expecting him to jump in the air to give a sideways kick
But never yet have I seen this trick
I do not know when he'll pass by
He never says, so I never ask why, his shoes they creak
It doesn't matter because his shoes do the talking
There's only a song, when he takes them walking.

Lynne O'Connor

NUMBERS

Numbers were my enemies at school.
Addition, subtraction,
multiplication and long-division
I struggled with hopelessly.
Later, fractions, geometry and algebra
compounded the problem,
crawling all over my page
at appointed times each week,
like difficult insects
you couldn't brush off.

I yearned for a world
free from decimal points,
that I might learn just where to place myself.
I knew numbers only from the outside,
but not what secrets lay within.

Calculating I'd be lighter by subtraction,
I offered my books to the solving fire.
I watched the air's disturbance as they burned,
and how everything was rendered,
slowly by degrees,
into harmless ash.

Stephen Paul

CIDER

What's the biggest difference
between Somerset and Devon?
Devon, it doesn't have much yeast,
Somerset has all the leaven.

For bushels and bushels of apples
grow on Somerset trees
and the air is full of sweetness
and the sweet attracts the bees.

And I would bet that Somerset bees
make honey that has the green
of lovely winding Somerset lanes
with the most flowers there've ever been

from the buttery yellow of buttercup
and pale cream of primrose
to the purple richness of thistle
and the wildness of the rose,

so the bees take up the pollen
and place it in the trees
and the cider waits in the apples
on branches as bent as old knees.

They droop heavy with cider apples
and the cider tastes of these,
these things that make up Somerset,
the earth, the hills, the meads.

The things that make cider sparkle,
the things that real cider needs.

Pam Redmond

First Snow

We wakened to a morning's dazzling light,
Where floating snowflakes fell like flowered rain.
Our world had changed from grey to pristine white
And icy patterns traced the frozen pane.
We braved the stair's numb cold with Arctic feet,
To find the roaring kitchen range below:
Then stood beside the fire's black-leaded heat
To store a little of that crimson glow
Before we faced the first fresh fall of winter's snow.

Janet L Smith

GOODBYE

You've disregarded it for a while
But today is now the day,
You'll have to say goodbye,
And let them go away.
They may be leaving your life,
But they'll never leave your heart,
They may be leaving your outside,
But inside you'll never be apart.
Time goes by and you're missing their affection,
You're feeling pain and you feel there's no connection.
There's only one thing I can say to you,
You know it's right and you know it's true.
It doesn't matter how long they've gone,
Or even where they are.
When you look out at the night,
They're looking at the same moon and stars.
Keep that in mind when you feel the bond has gone,
Love is immortal, it will always go on.

Rosanna Anstice

A Visit From Our Daughter

When our daughter comes to stay, everything is changed.
All my tidy cupboards are somehow rearranged.
I like to put our things away and shut the cupboard door,
But all she ever seems to do is leave things on the floor.

I need to make a phone call but the phone's not on the stand.
She rushes past and then I see the phone is in her hand.
Hurrah, at last it's my turn (my forehead feels quite wet)
But when it doesn't work, I know she's on the Internet.

'Are you doing any washing Mum?' (she's holding a big pile).
'Sorry, I've just finished mine,' I answer with a smile.
I see the mess around the house and think, *where can she be?*
I find her lying on the couch, watching the TV.

She never eats a meal with us as *we* have funny times!
Our evening meal is six o'clock, hers is half-past nine.
We go to bed, then she goes out. It's really such a pain
For then I stay up half the night till she comes home again.

Our dog is sleeping in her bed, I look on with despair,
For when she's gone it's me that has to clean up all the hair.
The time has passed and she has left (she has a flat in Spain)
Yet I know I won't be happy until she's back again.

Carole Ann Catt

THE OVERVIEW

The overview on life is perceived in a thousand minds
But no one can perceive it for what it truly is
Open-mindedness is not a gift we all possess
Dreams dreamed
But racism and homophobia still exist
Idealistic placed on words
But never moulded into reality
Dreams dreamed
But still the world remains the same.

Lou

WOMEN

When I think of women
My thoughts go to the telephone.
Both designed for speaking
Conveyors of gossip and talk-talk.
At the end of the day
You pick up the bill.
'La Donna mobile'
They are small in stature
With unpredictable output.
When considering the mouth-piece
That makes me think mother-in-law.
It's then I don my coat
And make for the nearest pub.
Later through a maudlin alcoholic haze
I do have to contend
When the telephone rings,
Although at times inconveniently irritating,
I'm irresistibly drawn
To giving it my full attention.

Robert Reddy

The Storm!

Black thunder clouds,
Scurried across the sky,
Rain pelted down,
Made everything far from dry.

The wind howled an angry song,
The trees whispered as they blew about.
Thunder clapped a big applause,
Lightning struck and a hurricane gave a shout.

The clouds spitted hail,
The world plunged into darkness,
As the last light of the sky faded,
How long will we be in greyness?

Our hearts began to lighten,
As the clouds began to brighten,
It's the sign the storm has broken,
Birds been woken, the dreaded storm spoken.

Gemma Musgrove

TOM AT TINTAGEL

Don't lean over the edge Tom:
These ancient walls built for arrows not boys to bounce.
The slurping, sucking tide may stretch and reach
With gravity in helpful tow.
But can you feel the strongest pull of all?
Don't lean over the edge Tom
Or the dark ages will get you!

Linda Bond

MILVERTON

Scent of roses, lavender and thyme
purr of the cat upon my knee.
Drone of bee and call of buzzard
the gentle sun upon my face.
Day of peace with time to rest,
Milverton summer, yes I am truly blessed.

Grazing cattle and fields of ripened corn,
this ancient village, weathered by the centuries,
enveloped by the peel of bells from
St Michael's Church, standing sentinel on the hill.

My garden looks down upon the lane
where friendly neighbours stop to chat.
A walk with my dog through the cider orchard
then back to my own little paradise
with a good book and a pot of tea.

I came to this village, a stranger,
but Milverton folk made me so welcome.
I feel as though I have been here forever.
Gentle village, kindly people, who make time
to stop and say hello.

Concerts, talks, so much to do and see.
Music and poetry, art and drama,
a wealth of talent this village holds.
Love and laughter, sadness and sorrow
all shared in a wealth of friendship.

Sylvie Johnstone

OUR SOMERSET 2004

The west of England, that's where'm to
Where cider reigns and 'Ow be you?'
'Good morning' - no - it's 'All right then?'
That greets you in the morning rain.
It's talk of country lores and fairs,
In language strange to foreign ears.
Of darts and carnivals and beer
And skittles at the 'Running Deer'.
We're farmers' men with hats of brown
And leggin's wand'ring through the town,
We know there's folk that think's us dumb
But can't pick elvers with their thumb.
The ditches, we all call 'em rines
They're deep and dirty, just like mines,
We makes our cheese, we brews our scrump
You 'ave too much, then you're a chump.
They call us yokels, say, 'Oo-ar!'
But can they sink a cider jar?
A time warp? Is that what they said?
With accent odd and faces red?
In Somerset we shall remain
The Yeomen of this fair terrain.

Robin Cherry

BLACKTHORN WINTER

The March day felt like winter as I wandered up the hill.
The sun was shining brightly but the north wind brought a chill.
The trees were bare and lifeless, with their leaves all blown away,
But dotted through the hedgerows, blackthorn blossom shone that day.

For all the cold north winds, the bumblebees were buzzing round,
And somehow spring was urging growth in new life from the ground.
Beside the lane the primroses were reaching for the sun
As in the field beyond the gate I watched the rabbits run.

The lambs were calling loudly in the orchards by the lane
And birds came down to drink in puddles made by last night's rain.
The hedgerows gave some shelter as the lane climbed up the hill
But when I reached the top, that biting wind was blowing still.

Along the hill, the nesting rooks were rising in the sky
To meet dark danger from above where buzzards circled high.
Below me on the levels, fields in glossy shades of green -
Between them rhynes were flowing with a lustrous silver sheen.

The Quantocks and the Blackdown Hills were distant shades of blue.
I stood there in that cold wind, taking in that splendid view.
Upon these Polden Hills, I'd found a place without compare
With blackthorn blossom in the hedge and birdsong in the air.

Penny Allwright

DEATH OF A ROMANCE

Sitting together in quality time, they gaze past each other
He reading his paper - her thoughts immersed in the wine.
They had such fun together in those halcyon days gone by,
Life's clouds but puffs of cotton wool against an azure sky.
The warmth of a smile and the tenderness of touch,
Private words and looks that had always meant so much.
Much joy and laughter surrounded family life.
Barometer set fair - no impending sense of strife.
Many years on and the storm clouds are brewing,
Skies have taken on a more threatening hue.
Cotton wool puffs are now just a memory -
Shades of grey have replaced the blue
Years have slipped by at increasing pace -
Lines of stress and time deeply etched on her face.
Her memories turn back the years to the young handsome man.
He hasn't changed much - her desire lingers on.
But why can't he see her as she was before? Desire her -
But to him she's a habit - alluring no more.
His hand that had held hers and felt always so pleasing,
Was now so perfunctory and needing a reason.
Yes, he loves her, but like a saggy, baggy old chair.
She's comfortable, he assumes she'll always be there.
But will she drift on? He had no way of knowing
The level to which her discontent was growing.
She was turning to someone who was leading the way
Down the path of fulfilment to a brighter new day.
So here she sits smiling - just biding her time.
He reading his paper - her thoughts immersed in the wine.

Jennie Gilbert

MIAOW MIAOW

This is the story of a black tomcat
who mostly spends his days lying on the mat!
A saucerful of milk, a dish of this and that,
a scratching pole, some fluffy toys
and a large cat flap.

Outside there was a garden
full of flowers and trees.
If black tomcat felt so inclined
he'd chase the birds and bees.

Sometimes he had a dish of cream
sometimes a fish's head.
He had a lovely mistress
and sometimes shared her bed.

His true love was the cat next door
a slinky sexy miss.
sometimes she'd let him get quite close,
sometimes she'd scratch and hiss.

She was a moody sulky cat
old black Tom couldn't cope.
She sat upon the dustbin lid
her tail lashed like a rope.

Another day she'd purr and stretch
as pleasant as can be.
Black Tom he'd played his cards just right
and asked her in for tea.

They shared a bowl of richest cream
and ate a big fish pie.
They curled together on the mat
there'll be kittens by and by.

Violet Higgins

THE KITE

A windy day and high on a hill
A boy flies his kite,
The wind is strong.
He pulls, let's go and pulls again
With all his might.
Up, up goes the kite,
Bobbing and weaving round the sky.
Its colours bright in the sun,
Streamers giving to the wind.
The boy is having fun.

Doris M Miller

CIRCLES

One more day
Just hours old, but
Sleepless weeks have made it weary.
Has it really just begun?
Still the sun rises.
Restlessness.

Losing the fight
But can't give up.
Try to forget, though always aware;
No rest now as pain blurs dreams.
Feeling, denying, pretending.

Striving, grasping, falling.

So much to feel
That time slows down.
Crushing intensity of thoughts
Hurts all over. Emotions strong;
Expression fails. They're
Locked inside.

Striving, grasping, fallen.

Almost restored; never the same.
Battle scars are reminders of
Emotional surgery
Needed to bring change;
Caused by change.

Estelle Ann Emily Jackson

SOMERSET 2004 - SOMERSET IN SHORT

Arable ground
The flowers in bud
Swans swim around
The moors in flood

Old tranquil lanes
Hectic rush hours
Brass weather vanes
On fine church towers

Cricket matches
The churchyard fétes
Bright sunlight catches
Wrought iron gates

Rustic fruit farms
Old traditions
Signpost arms
Superstitions

Fresh seaside air
The hillside view
Bridgwater Fair
Autumnal dew

Bonfire nights
Firework displays
Carnival lights
All make our days

Yeovil to Minehead
Wells to Liscombe
Frome to Nynehead
Crewkerne to Triscombe

Somerset county
Creation's bounty.

Paul Spender

THE PROMISE

This photograph
Wrinkles along a fold
To fit my wallet
Sunshine spills from
Its faded image

He is the Adonis
Chest smooth and tanned
The island holiday brochure
He is laughing
Head tipped back
Public schoolboy hair
Golden and unruly

His leg has threaded through hers
Brown and white skin entwined
The sea wind trespasses
The space between her knees
Her dress hem dances
At its invitation

She is looking at me
The spell of her eyes tamed beneath her hat
Dark deep curls escape
Below its brim

She is looking at me
And she strokes me
With her smile
As wide and glorious
As our beach

R Bryant

A Computer Widow

Most men like to have a hobby of sorts,
This can be anything but usually sports.
Cricket, football, tennis, golf or snooker,
But my husband's hobby is his computer.

Upstairs on the computer, every night,
I told him straight, this just isn't right.
Being downstairs with my own company,
When the two of us should be in harmony.

If you can't beat them join them, the saying goes
And I was determined to get into the throes.
I told him I wanted to learn about the computer,
'Will you help me?' I asked. 'Please be my tutor.'

So now the two of us are as happy as can be,
We can talk in computer jargon you see.
I think he's really clever being able to teach me,
He thinks I'm clever because I'm finding it easy.

Rosemary Davies

The Engagement

Suddenly, unexpectedly
Possibility blooms into reality
The path of life is altered forever
A spring of emotions, hopes and dreams bubbles into life
With increasing and unstoppable speed,
Their chance to takeover has been seized

Love grows, unfolds
Acknowledges the touch of life's endless cycles
The inescapable joy
Validation, security, adventure
Caring for another
Sharing with another,
Fear perched on the crest of the wave

Uncertainty accepted
Risk swells into being
Speculation magnifying into hugeness
Fortunes remain unknown in the vastness
A journey filled with treasure prevailing over heartache
A ring to witness the passing of time

Anabel Green

Sister Dear

My sister is a delight
I sometimes think she's not right
To leave her children stranded
Whilst she goes single handed
To explore sunny climes.

She irons for a living
But that is always giving
Her a backache sure to cripple
And then she needs a tipple
Of her favourite wine.

And though she'll soon be fifty
She's still so very nifty
As she struts the disco dances
And gets the 'Come on' glances
From the hunky younger guys.

Her dearest sport is jogging
I wonder if she's flogging
A dead horse now she's older
She tripped and strained her shoulder
When she fell on her knees.

Beverly Maiden

LIFE'S JOURNEY

I stood at a crossroads, didn't know which way to turn.
The day was spent, the night was dark, no light seemed to burn.
I stood and waited silently; my heart was full of fear.
I was scared, yes *terrified,* then a voice said - 'I am here.'

I looked around; saw no one there, yet felt I was not alone.
My fears just went, the way was clear, as though a light was shown.
I took the way thus lit for me; I found it narrow - straight.
I stumbled on the best I could, through sorrow, love and hate.

The path at times was stony; I tripped, had many a fall.
Got up each time to fall again, I finally had to crawl.
I cried out with my efforts. 'Won't someone help me, *please?'*
The voice again said, 'I am here - now get up off your knees.'

'Be brave my son. Have faith in me.' That voice went on to say,
'Just reach right out and take my hand, I'll guide you on your way.'
I stretched out into the darkness, I found nobody there.
But still I felt His presence; it was in the very air.

I carried on right through the night until I saw the dawn.
I looked for him who'd walked with me; to no avail, my heart was torn.
But then I heard him whisper more, 'If you would be my friend,
do for others, as I've done for you. Guide them to their journey's end.'

Brian Muchmore

URBAN HUNTER GATHERER

I'm an urban hunter gatherer,
I live by wits alone,
An urban hunter gatherer,
The streets I call my home.

An urban hunter gatherer,
I endure by sense and stealth,
An urban hunter gatherer,
I envy you your wealth.

An urban hunter gatherer
No family or friends,
An urban hunter gatherer
Martyr of social trends.

An urban hunter gatherer,
I melt into the crowd,
An urban hunter gatherer
No job to make me proud.

An urban hunter gatherer,
Who once was more than this,
An urban hunter gatherer,
No chance of wedded bliss.

An urban hunter gatherer,
Looked down on and deplored,
An urban hunter gatherer
Society ignores.

An urban hunter gatherer,
Who wishes he were dead,
An urban hunter gatherer,
Who could be you instead.

Mark Sherborne

BELLEVER SUMMER

This I will remember,
The shade of trees
And grass seared by the sun -
Fish leaping
Caught in silver light,
Indigo dragonflies and
Weed water flowing
Towards brooding rocks.
Children with nets
Under the high sky of summer;
A mare and foal
Coming to drink on thrusting feet.
All this I will remember,
And when memory
For other things has gone,
This too I will remember -
Your face and our sweet loving
Underneath the sun.

D M Neu

SEPIA GIANTS

My grandad took that photograph. Eleven village men,
his proudly staring sepia team of summer nineteen-ten,
who lived as custom ordered them and touched their caps to Squire,
who sat in church in stiff serge suits and worked and died in mire.
Eleven faded summer men caught in a camera's flash,
now, curled on the pavilion wall, still cut their nameless dash.
But who will find our present team so honourable a place?
Weekenders who have bought us cheap and scrubbed our rural face,
and torn up cottage gardens, laying concrete to their doors
for easy space in which to park their city 4 x 4's;
whose rural idyll bristles with alarms and double locks;
who've priced my children's children into distant tower blocks,
while each drives off when stumps are drawn to sit beside his pool
at The Granary, Old Bakery, Old Stables and Old School,
past the names of Grandad's giants on a tall cross in the square
while the sepia ghosts of nineteen-ten, uncomprehending, stare.

Martin Parker

HEALTHY AND FREE, THE WORLD WAS BEFORE US!

The Triangle Holiday Club, Perforce
A group of friends in a Plymouth City coach,
Set out from Woodford in Devon.
Their destination proved to be
The very stairway to Heaven.

To Gateshead in England, they repaired,
Heading for the North Sea,
The friendly Geordies set them up with friendship and food,
                                                                                                                    well prepared,
The vessel, MS Jupiter, seaworthy, proved to be.

The Port of Bergen received them well
The journey commenced to the Stalheim Hotel.
The awesome wonders, Fjord and waterfall, the red lady of Flamme
Captured the hearts of one and all.

The colour of water, the Riverdance,
The trees themselves expressing the miracle of creation,
Their foliage and movement, the power and the glory,
Tell their own story.

The 'Folk Night' at a family hotel,
Musicians in National dress, hose and garters,
Toe tapping and clapping, the fiddlers encouraged us well.
Alas persuaded, we couldn't agree,
The Riverdance to perform, rheumatics prevailed,
It was outside our every day norm.

Nor the 'Blue Tango' from another time, in another place,
The melodious strains from piano grand,
A quickstep or two, yes that we could do
It was like Billy Cotton's band!

What with dancing and swimming, shopping, laughing and eating,
Too quickly the holiday passed.
Enjoyed ourselves very much did we
'To Tuscany next year?' we asked.

Beryl Moorehead

STILL DEVON

I'm from Devon
On a limb
The motorway
Stops halfway in,

This laid back county
Quiet and still
With farmers early
Fields to till,

Such views of plenty
Fill your mind
This peaceful life
Still so refined,

This land of Devon
On a limb
But once you're here
You'll stay within.

James L Wood

Full Circle

My granny, Hannah Mary, born eighteen seventy
In Devon's salty Salcombe near the clear Custom House Quay
Married young, a sailor who sailed the seven seas
In the handsome Adelaide Mary, bringing citrus fruits to please

Her first son Oscar, born at home, weighed just eleven pounds!
The doctor came out late on horseback on his rounds
No in-patient monitoring then, no underwater birth
Granny's girlish waist assumed a grander girth

They had six babes all told, two died young and went to Heaven
But Oscar was the only one born in County Devon
For engines replaced sails in bigger ships with funnels
Which blew out smoke and steam - foghorned across the gunwales

And such were built elsewhere in special huge dry docks
In ports like Liverpool, my home, where seagulls flew in flocks
So Granny had to move to a back street terrace house
In the port of Liverpool - but she never was a Scouse

She kept her Devon accent until the day she died
And always talked of Salcombe with longing, love and pride
People travelled little then but she went back once - to be
Disgusted at the washing hanging out along the Quay!

I'm sad she died so long before I came to live in Devon
I know somewhere she's pleased I've found her earthly heaven

I loved the docks of Liverpool where my father toiled
But the waters of the Mersey got silted up and spoiled
The shipping work has gone, the buildings all converted
To be upmarket properties, never to be reverted

So - after more than forty years of Torrington May Fair
And 'Uz be plaized to see 'ee' strung out across The Square
Tho I'll never be a local . . . This is home, my heart is here
Throw back two generations: oh thank you Granny dear!

V Jean Tyler

RETURN TO DEVON

Bideford
The ten year interval displays
Our family's growth and change.
I see this in the photographs:
Less innocence; more range.

Bideford keeps sleepy charm:
Perhaps more cut-off and run down:
But gloriously still, Victoria Park
Bejewels the cream-walled Torridge town;

And this repays the screaming time
It takes, by motor, to arrive;
North Devon: Taunton knows you not:
You rate no path from the M5.

Instow
The ten years here had played me tricks:
Was our house this far from the sand?
I climbed the dunes and scanned the Taw
Till recognition came to hand.

And all returned: the Tarka Trail;
Promontory with cricket ground;
Lundy Island - on a clear day;
Braunton Air Show's booming sound;

White walls, grey roofs of Appledore
Across the bay the Torridge spans;
And then the area's finest crown:
Much-loved: the Hocking's ice cream vans!

Jerry Dowlen

THE FRONTLINE

Hell!
The curse of death gushes through the air
Rows of silent men gallantly prepare
Dropping like snowflakes from starlit skies
To fields filled with battle, thuds, bullets and cries

Reality hits with suffocating sounds of death
Frontline duty, comrade's last breath
Crawling through sodden fields of mud
Head bowed low from machine gun's thirst for blood

The rancid smell of burning flesh and gunpowder smoke
Stench of fear, breathe or choke
The whistle of a bomb, scream of a shell
Sixty years on this is still my *hell!*

R S Wayne Hughes

SPECIAL MOMENTS

There was a moment
When you walked into the room
And my heart skipped a beat,
When I first saw you.

There was a moment
When you held me in your arms,
We kissed and I trembled
At our first embrace.

There was a moment
When we made our vows
And I felt warm inside
As we two became as one.

There was a moment
When our child was born
And I cried tears of joy
For that special gift.

There was a moment
When you passed away,
My heart missed a beat, I trembled
And I cried tears of sorrow at our parting.

Dawn Woon

BLESSINGS

I walked up Wild Flower lane,
All is peace and tranquillity.
I find it hard going, up the hill,
Not as young as I used to be!
The hedgerows are very pretty,
Wild Michaelmas Daisies,
Campion, a beautiful cerise colour,
Bluebells, white May blossom,
Yellow buttercups and little white daisies.
Intertwined with the hedgerow were cultivated flowers,
That had pushed their way through the garden fences.
All was pleasing to the eye.
I could hear the birds singing,
All the hedgerows seemed to be alive,
Yet peaceful.
The sun was shining, there was a slight breeze,
In my lonely state, (I am now a widow)
It seemed like paradise.
We are blessed in so many ways,
It is still good to be alive.

Olive Young

PERRANUTHNOE

Softly, swaying gorse
sings to Atlantic swells; the sky is clear.

Come, step into the scullery
Percy Curnow may take us fishing; he knows the sea.
If we are lucky we will have mackerel for our tea.
Saffron
Starch
Slate
Sea
Blow softly, softly through me

Pastry worms, empty shells.
Ding-dong, detached
Look into the water; water filled, serene.
Saffron
Starch
Slate
Sea
Blow softly, softly to me

Softly, swaying gorse stings on tiny knees.
Meandering days, daily hours. Sarazin piles.
Ding-dong; let them in.
Come on in.
Halycon flowers
Withered myths
Smouldering embers on a midnight fire

Saffron
Starch
Slate
Sea
Drifting slowly from me.

Sallie Boothman

IN-BETWEEN TIMES

I love the in-between times,
not the real times, mean times or serene times,
nor the dream times, keen times or lean times,
it's the in-between times I love.

I love the time between the day and night,
the gap between what is wrong and what's right.
I love the space between desire and hate,
the world between our choice and fate.

I love the in-between times,
not the grave times, hot times or cold times,
nor the brave times, feared times or bold times,
it's the in-between times I love.

I love the place between present and past,
the freedom between the first and the last.
I love the delay between dreams and day,
the tiers between what we think and say.

I love the in-between times,
not the hard times, down times or dark times,
nor the good times, fun times or stark times,
it's the in-between times I love.

I love the seconds between birth and death,
the pause between your kisses and breath.
I love the blur between the land and sea,
these strange mysteries between you and me.

Alan M Kent

WELCOME TO CORNWALL

Two old folk strolled happily over the downs it was evening and just
after tea, they looked at the beach and the miles of grassland
and the cliffs dropping down to the sea,
'Oh isn't this great lass,' the old fellow said,
'just think if we only lived here I would walk across here every day
of my life - I would even take you for a beer.'

She reached for his hand then he gave her a hug
as they stood there and watched the sun set,
I hurried on by looking up to the sky,
my excuse was the trail of a 'jet'.
It was later that week that I stopped there and looked,
from the very same spot they had found,
what a marvellous scene I'd not seen it before
I was too busy rushing around.

We go thousands of miles for the sunshine
to see things in all foreign lands,
we are seasick and get 'gippy-tummy'
sometimes we can't bathe from the sands,
let's walk half a mile and be happy
and look at the beauty that's here -
and welcome the visitors for their two short weeks
- because we have it all of the year.

The carnival's gone and the Jazz Week
the beaches and golf course are clear
there is space now to swim or go playing,
or fish from the cliff or the pier;
the hotels are closing and staff plan their break -
they know that the season is done
maybe soak up the sun in faraway lands
then come back next year for our sun.

It now is October the summer has gone
and most of the car parks are free -
have we all wished for this for six months or more
or was it for just the last three?
the roads are all empty, the people have gone
as over the pavements we roam,
the shops are all quiet and tills lose their ring
as visitors wend their way home.

The nights are much longer the days are too short,
we can't even walk after tea -
the winter is here, then it's Christmas,
when bells and tills ring merrily.
Did we *really* wish summer to go rushing by
and take away birds and the flowers,
of course we did not, it is just modern life
that makes us count days just as hours.

Jim Pritchard

TO KILL A FOX

I can think of several ways
To kill a fox.
How about releasing poisonous fumes
Into the fox hole,
So that the animal is quietly gassed
Before choking to death.
That's not bad, is it?
At least there are no marks on the body,
No torn limbs or mangled fur.
Or try putting poison down.
Oh, spare him from that.
So let's shoot him,
Though we may only maim him,
And leave him to crawl away
To die a lingering death.
But finally, of course
'Tally Ho!' let's chase him
With a pack of hounds,
And the thundering of horses' hooves.
When he is finally cornered,
The hounds can have their sport
And tear him limb from limb.
Their barking muffling his screams.
But foxes are vermin.
They kill the farmers' stock,
So must be destroyed,
In spite of being God's creatures.
We all know how to kill foxes,
But not nicely.
Dear God, that is impossible, isn't it?

Eve M Turner

SELF DEFENCE

He acted like an animal tonight
I reach for the bottle unscrewing the lid
Laying them out on the table
I don't understand what I did.

He has hurt and humiliated me
He has never been this bad before
I can't take his short fuse any longer
He has made me feel so insecure.

Why should I end my life?
When it's scum like him that should go
Taking all the fear and suffering with him
For once he can suffer the blow.

Picking up the knife
Its edge shining in the light
I approach the place in which he's sat
This will teach him next time not to fight.

With a terrifying force
I plunge the knife into his sorry skull
The blood-curdling scream ringing in my ears
Then the deadly silence, unforgettable.

With my anger boiling
And rage racing through me
I repeatedly slice him, slashing his face
Scraping out his eyes to stop him to see.

I furiously butcher him
Making him pay for the torment he caused me
Then exhausted I sit on the blood soaked sofa
And hold his shredded body close to me.

Kailie Old (16)

THE ALL NIGHT DINER

In the all night diner that is
Texan death row the fries
are hot tonight with chicken
wings and spicy things fajitas
for the underclass it's
KFC and literacy prepare
to meet your maker and if it
needs some stelazine chlorpromazine and
buns to wash it down and
make it sane in order it
can die again the lesson
learned for other blacks with
low IQs and chequered slacks the
fast food's frying at the Texan
barbecue your maker waits
again to don his white and flaming
mask just to cauterise and
circumcise you

Give me a stake to
pierce the white vampiric
heart

Give me a stake and
help to drive it
home.

David Waddilove

HOLLOW LAUGHTER

It is just an ugly rumour
That men have a sense of humour;
They're full of anecdotes and smutty tales.
But let a woman make a pun
And they lose all sense of fun.
You see, a sense of humour's only meant for *males*.

I have stood amidst a horde
Of Alpha Males - and been ignored
When I've made a rather witty repartee;
Within minutes of my joke
It's repeated by some bloke
As though he's made it up himself - not *me*.

But I put it down to age
And restrain my rightful rage;
We women must not boast our natural wit
Or our image-conscious menfolk
Might feel threatened by their henfolk -
But they're going to have to learn to live with it!

Jane Clarke

SLEEPLESS

Windy, gusty, rain and clouds
Night-time lingers
Spirit's finger
Spooky, creaky, laying meekly
All around
The strangest sounds
Shadows dancing
Goblins prancing
Evil feeling
Not revealing
Sight nor sound
Waking endless
Turning thinking
Eyes are blinking
Inward shrinking
Hearing every sound
Sleep unheeded
Badly needed
Thoughts escaping
Continued waking
Morning breaking
Overtaking
Normality is found.

Jacqueline Briggs

CONVERSATION WITH A TREE

Do you realise?
Oh ancient tree
Generations stood under you
And looked up to see.

Oh have mercy,
As I stand so bold,
Look up and see,
I'm very old.

I gaze up at your canopy,
Oh ancient being,
They shan't fell you,
You're better seen.

I lean with age,
Looks quite odd,
But my trunk stands firm,
In fertile sod.

A beautiful bark,
A textured shell,
How very splendid,
Your flowers smell.

Oh I say in reply,
You will grow old
And lay in my meadows,
If truth were told.

But I have you know,
A you look up to me,
The day will come,
You'll lay under me.

Talmadge Rogalla

SUBMISSIONS INVITED
SOMETHING FOR EVERYONE

OVER £10,000 POETRY PRIZES TO BE WON!

POETRY NOW 2004 - Any subject, any style, any time.

WOMENSWORDS 2004 - Strictly women, have your say the female way!

STRONGWORDS 2004 - Warning! Opinionated and have strong views. (Not for the faint-hearted)

All poems no longer than 30 lines.
Always welcome! No fee!
Cash Prizes to be won!

Mark your envelope (eg *Poetry Now*) **2004**
Send to:
Forward Press Ltd
Remus House, Coltsfoot Drive,
Peterborough, PE2 9JX
(01733) 898101

If you would like to order further copies of this book or any of our other titles, please give us a call or log onto our website at
www.forwardpress.co.uk